Other Side of This Trial

My Story, His Plan, His Hand

by Billy Gaines

Help me, O Lord my God! Oh, save me according to Your mercy, that they may know that this is Your hand—that You, Lord, have done it!
Psalm 109:26-27

Eternal Heiress

Publishing

Eternal Heiress Publishing, Nashville, TN
Copyright © 2023 by Billy Gaines

Cover Design & Page Design: Bayley Holt
Editing: Ashley Hagan
Paperback ISBN: 9798985693423
eBook ISBN: 979-8-9856934-3-0

Praise for *Other Side of this Trial*

I think you will be blessed by *Other Side of This Trial* written by my dear friend Billy Gaines. The event-by-event evidence of the hand of God working on his behalf clearly illustrates the fruit of a life yielded and trusting in the goodness, mercy, guidance, and power of God.

—Kathie Lee Gifford, Emmy-award winning host, actress, singer, and songwriter

I have dedicated my life to sharing the message of Jesus Christ and spreading God's love with others, and when I find people whose purpose in life is the same, I hold on to them with my heart. It has been my absolute pleasure to meet and get to interview Billy Gaines about the miracles that have happened in his life. I have had the opportunity to interview hundreds of people on my radio show, and there is something so special about Billy's passion, experiences, and love.

Singer, songwriter, author, speaker, and minister Billy Gaines is an all-around motivator and missionary. It is his calling to preach the gospel of Jesus Christ, and he does exactly that in every aspect of his life. Through his music, songwriting, and ministry Billy Gaines has inspired and changed the lives of millions, and he's continuing to do that through his book, *Other Side of This Trial*. Through captivating stories of Billy's life, we're reminded that the true path to happiness and success is the one in which the Lord leads you. This book is captivating, it will bring you to tears, and it will encourage you to follow your God-given path.

I congratulate Billy on this beautifully written account of his life, his experiences, his love, and his passion, and I appreciate Billy sharing those stories with us in *Other Side of This Trial*.

—Irlene Mandrell, singer, actress, author, and radio personality

To know Billy Gaines is to know a humble servant of deep faith; to hear Billy is to experience an anointed artist with a smooth, soulful voice that has captivated audiences for more than three decades. Readers will discover the godly legacy of generations that shaped this man as well as the R&B and Gospel roots that captured his heart to pursue his God-given talents. Through the high notes and the low notes, Billy continually lives in the grace notes, reminding us that God has orchestrated every key. Similarly, he invites the reader to examine their own life and look for the Master's guiding Hand.

—Candace Kirkpatrick, actress, speaker, producer

Other Side of this Trial by Billy Gaines invites readers on a profound journey through the remarkable intersections of faith, personal anecdotes, and divine interventions. This Christian book is a heartfelt exploration of how faith can sustain and uplift, even in the face of life's greatest challenges.
—**Dr. Marie Cosgrove, international speaker and author of** *Greater Fortune: Essential Lessons from the Entrepreneur Who Bought the Company that Fired Her.*

It is an honor for me to write an endorsement for my dear friend, Billy Gaines. Billy is a man who is in relentless pursuit of the Lord. You will see the endurance and patience of this pursuit as you read the pages of this book. I have not only seen Billy's enduring pursuit of God written on the pages of this book, but I have seen it up close and personal, written upon his heart. I have stood beside Billy's side and prayed with him as his wife Christy was passing into eternity. I have watched his character as he walked through many trials and sufferings that would typically knock out the strongest of men. Billy's relentless passion for Christ has made him strong in faith and forged the character of Christ in his life. As you read this book, listen to the Holy Spirit's gentle voice, and be challenged to stay steady in the hard times of life!
— **Pastor Dave Allman, New Life Church, Poland, Ohio**

Billy Gaines' new book, *Other Side of This Trial,* is a captivating read that shares inspiring testimonies from his childhood, music career, family complications, health issues, financial needs, romance, and more. Gaines' passion for music, songwriting, ministry, and family shines through the pages, making it a relatable and heartwarming read. The book is set in the Nashville church culture, and Gaines' stories about local pastors, musicians, and leaders make it feel like you're right there with him. The falling in love story is especially captivating, and it's hard not to be moved by the emotional impact of the book. Gaines' relatable stories and "God nods" will make you giggle, while his real-life experiences will bring you to tears. If you're looking for inspiration and faith-building testimonies, *Other Side of This Trial* is a must-read. Don't miss out on this incredible book—grab your copy today!
—**Angel Faulk, The Fitness Angel, health coach, fitness expert, author, and speaker**

Other Side of This Trial is a touching memoir telling of God's miraculous interventions and interactions in Billy's life that spans generations. As the author beautifully wrote, "We must be mindful of and purposely remember the things God has done in our lives. They are evidence of His presence, His power, and His very existence." This encouraging book is a great read and reminder to us all that whether experiencing joy on the mountain tops of life or walking through the hard valleys, God is always present, ever interceding on our behalf.
—**G.L. Mendenhall, author of** *Angels in Our Room*

To my children Rachel, Jason, and Nathan, my
son-in-law Brian, and my grandchildren Olivia and Briley.

Table of Contents

Introduction

A man's heart plans his way, but the Lord directs his steps.
Proverbs 16:9

This book is not a full autobiography, but rather a memoir of miraculous interventions that defy statistical probability. It is a chronicle of gratitude, born out of reminding myself daily of the goodness of God. My life story is filled with instances of unimaginable protection, provision, and guidance that might lead someone to think it's fictional. It is also an account of sorrows so deep it would seem there was a cosmic conspiracy to destroy me with sadness. But in the good times as well as the sorrowful times, I have found the pleasantly surprising and unforeseen purpose of the mighty and loving hand of God.

I was inspired to write this book after I received a Father's Day gift from my daughter Rachel, her husband Brian, and their children, Olivia and Briley. The title of the book they gave me was *Grandpa Tell Me Your Memories* by Kathleen Lashier, and it was a daily journal for me to record my childhood memories.

As I began answering the daily questions in the journal, I was inspired to go a step further and give a more detailed account of my life, particularly the events where God showed Himself mighty on my behalf. I found myself rejoicing in the blessings God has given me as He has fulfilled the call and purpose for my life, and I was struck by the realization that He was orchestrating my life even before I was born. In a phone conversation with my sister Barbara, I began to share the miraculous interventions of the Lord, and she said, "The hand of God." As I shared one story after another, we both began to say together, "The hand of God." The focus of my book was born.

So, after many false starts, my hopes and longings for sharing my story finally came together. This book is the result.

Family History of Faith

*I thank God, whom I serve with a pure conscience, as my
forefathers did, as without ceasing I remember you in my
prayers night and day, greatly desiring to see you, being mindful
of your tears, that I may be filled with joy, when I call to
remembrance the genuine faith that is in you, which dwelt first
in your grandmother Lois and your mother Eunice, and I am
persuaded is in you also. Therefore, I remind you to stir up the
gift of God which is in you through the laying on of my hands.
For God has not given us a spirit of fear, but of power and of
love and of a sound mind.*
II Timothy 1:3-7

I'm absolutely certain that I would not be the person I am in the Lord if it were not for the foundation of the prayers of my ancestors. Everything from my paternal grandfather's prayers that all his descendants would serve God, to the teaching of my parents, to the words of affirmation from my maternal grandfather, has made a foundational contribution to my spiritual making. Some of the lyrics from my song "The Part that No One Sees" express this sentiment:

A faithful saint kneels down before the Lord behind closed doors
Desire for others' welfare is outpoured
Mighty bonds are broken by those simple, selfless prayers
While victors stand in victory unaware

There is something I like to call spiritual DNA. What I mean by that is there are certain spiritual characteristics that are gifts to us, passed down from one generation to another. This is clearly referenced by the apostle Paul when he mentions that he served God with a pure conscience as his forefathers did. Secondly, he mentions to Timothy that the faith that was in him first abided in his grandmother Lois and in his mother Eunice. Thirdly, he references that there was a gift in Timothy to be stirred up, which had been given by the laying on of Paul's hands. There was also a prophetic utterance concerning him that needed to be stirred up so that he could "wage a good warfare" (1 Timothy 1:18). The concept of physical touch and passing on giftings, blessings, and callings is very real. I am truly grateful to be a recipient of this spiritual transfer and to know that now I am surrounded by a great cloud of witnesses. By that I don't mean only my own ancestors, but all of God's people whose lives are evidence of the surety of what God has promised by their faith and belief in the face of adversity.

When we pass the torch of spiritual understanding, it's not passive; it is an active delivery of that legacy. It requires deliberate effort to ensure that the truth we know and have experienced from the hand of God ourselves is passed on to generations to come. My children heard me mention the terminology of "your children and your children's children" so many times that they came up with a little joke. They would say, "Your children's children and your children's children's children." Passing along the knowledge of the wonderful works God has done in a previous generation and the knowledge of His commandments is essential for the encouragement, enlightenment, and instruction of future generations.

Hear, O Israel: The Lord our God, the Lord is one! You shall
love the Lord your God with all your heart, with all your soul,

and with all your strength. And these words which I command
you today shall be in your heart. You shall teach them diligently
to your children, and shall talk of them when you sit in your
house, when you walk by the way, when you lie down, and when
you rise up. You shall bind them as a sign on your hand, and
they shall be as frontlets between your eyes. You shall write them
on the doorposts of your house and on your gates.

Deuteronomy 6:4-9

Lavinia Johnson

My earliest known Christian relative is my
mother's paternal grandmother. She was born
into slavery in 1857, and was eight years old at the
end of the Civil War. I grew up with this portrait
hanging in our living room, and I humorously
thought the handle of the fan looked like a
gigantic matchstick! This photo was taken when
she was in her twenties. She was one of seven
freed slaves who were founding members of St.
John Baptist Church in the Washington Park area of Richmond, VA. Her
son, Harvey Hampton Johnson (my grandfather), was the choir director
for St. John Baptist Church for many years. His sister, Betty (my great
aunt), was the organist for the church and director of the youth choir I was
a part of at one point.

Papa's Prayers and Tears

The earliest evidence I have of God's plan for my life happened before I
was born. It's a story from my father, Herman S. Gaines Sr., that my brother
Jonathan told me after my father died. As a boy, my father was standing in
front of his father, William Henry Allen Gaines, staring up at him while
he prayed. He heard him pray and ask that all his descendants would serve

God. As he prayed, tears rolled down his cheeks and fell from his face into my father's face as he was looking up at him. It was as if this was a generational anointing of tears. Though my grandfather died before I was born, I know that my walk with the Lord, along with that of his other descendants who served the Lord, are in part a result of Papa's prayers and tears.

Tears are more than just water that pours from our eyes and runs on our face. They are so important to God that He keeps a record of them (Psalm 56:8). He has promised to one day wipe all our tears away, and there will be no more crying: "And God will wipe away every tear from their eyes; there shall be no more death, nor sorrow, nor crying. There shall be no more pain, for the former things have passed away" (Revelation 21:4). The tears and prayers of my grandfather created a legacy of faith in my family, and I am confident that the addition of my own tears and prayers will continue that legacy to my children and grandchildren.

Daddy's Miracle

In March 1933, the U.S. Congress established the Civilian Conservation Corps as a relief program for unmarried young men between the ages of eighteen and twenty-five. Within three months, 250,000 men had enrolled. The Civilian Conservation Corps (CCC) proved to be one of the most popular programs in President Franklin Delano Roosevelt's New Deal program. The program's goal was to conserve the country's natural resources while providing jobs for young men. In 1935, at age eighteen, my father was one of them.

My father's family lived on Seldon Street in the Church Hill neighborhood of Richmond, Virginia. One day, he was called home from CCC camp because his mother, Mary Gaines, had fallen gravely ill. When he walked into the bedroom, he saw his mother lying in a catatonic state, unresponsive, with her eyes fixed in the upper left corner of the bedroom. He screamed and fell to his knees with his head on the edge of the bed. With tears pouring from his eyes, he cried out, "God, please save my mama!

If you save my mama, I will serve you all the days of my life."

While he was still there weeping and kneeling, Grandma Gaines reached out her right hand and placed it on his head. "Herman?" she asked. The happiness that filled the room that day would become legendary, a story repeatedly told generation after generation. But even more than that, it was a tangible, faith-building manifestation of the hand of God.

Grandma Gaines with my cousin Farley Woodridge and my sister Barbara

Remarkably, Grandma Gaines would live another thirty years. I can still remember the day my father came and told me she had died. I was six years old at the time, and I don't remember her funeral, but I do remember very distinctly my father standing next to her casket at her graveside, weeping.

This story was irrefutable evidence to me of God's amazing power to heal. It showed me that He does indeed hear our impassioned cries. I know that God doesn't heal in every situation, and though I don't have an explanation for why, I still believe it is undeniable that God moves on behalf of a fervent, effectual prayer. Whatever the reasoning behind the seeming inconsistency of miraculous manifestation, it is by faith that we press on and continue to believe that every time we lay hands on someone, they will be healed. We hold onto hope in the face of unlikeliness or impossibility. Despite unanswered prayer, disappointment, or frustrated expectations, I still face every life situation believing that with God all things are possible (Matthew 19:26).

In the Womb

I almost didn't make it into the world! My mother was involved in a car accident while pregnant with me. My father was driving, and my mother was riding in the passenger seat. These were the days before seatbelts, and the collision hurled her belly-first into the dashboard. I was knocked sideways in her womb so that her baby bump was sticking out to her right side. She did not go into labor at the time, and I'm not sure whether this accident contributed to me being a "dry birth" baby when I did come into the world. I was basically born dehydrated, and as my mother described me, "wrinkled like a prune." Whatever the case, this accident could easily have been fatal for me. My very survival shows me the protective hand of God on my life.

I can't help but be reminded of the fact that when I was in my mother's womb, God knew me. And in that womb, he protected me. The fact that I was not severely injured leads me to believe that the angel of the Lord indeed was watching over me, keeping me from harm because of the purpose that God had planned for my life.

> *For You formed my inward parts; You covered me in my mother's womb. I will praise You, for I am fearfully and wonderfully made; marvelous are Your works, and that my soul knows very well. My frame was not hidden from You, when I was made in secret, and skillfully wrought in the lowest parts of the earth. Your eyes saw my substance, being yet unformed. And in Your book they all were written, the days fashioned for me, when as yet there were none of them.*
> Psalm 139:13-16

Saved by Aunt Barbara

My cousin Wanda Falden has laughingly reminded me through the years of another "in the womb" story. My aunt Barbara Falden was my mother Lavinia's baby sister. She was pregnant with my cousin Wanda when this incident occurred. I'm not sure just how old I was, but I think I was close to the age of two. She and my mother were outside with me, and as my Aunt Barbara put it, I was "doing what little adventurous boys do."

I ran toward a puddle of muddy water I had spotted in the middle of the street. A car was approaching, and Aunt Barbara took off running after me to keep me from getting killed. She caught me, but in the process she fell on her pregnant belly, endangering my cousin Wanda in the womb. Without even thinking of the risk, Aunt Barbara saved my life. She said that Wanda "turned every way but loose that night" in her womb.

Aunt Barbara's selfless act was once again evidence to me of the hand of God in action. It was so perfectly timed, and my Aunt Barbara was so perfectly positioned to grab me back in time, just before a car hit me, that it could only have been God intervening. I believe that if it wasn't for God sending His angels to protect children from their own foolish actions, there would be many more funerals planned all over this world!

White-Gloved Hand

When I was three, my dad took me with him to a store on Broad Street in downtown Richmond. Daddy had gone into the store for just a few minutes and left me in the front seat. This was long before modern controversies about leaving a child in a car. It was a practice that many parents thought little of in those days. When he came out of the store, he saw a Caucasian woman walking down the sidewalk with me in her arms, rubbing my hairless head with a white-gloved hand. I am not sure whether she was walking away or toward him, but he was quite upset about it, and asked the lady, "What are you doing with my baby?"

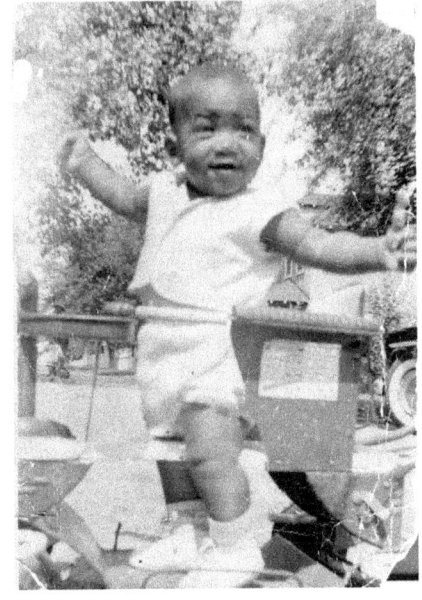

She told Daddy she had seen

me walking down the sidewalk alone and scooped me up. My father replied that there was no way I could have unlocked the door, operated the door handle, and had the strength to open a car door. He believed she had reached into the car through the open window and taken me out of the front seat.

I thought about this story for many years, and it's hard for me to believe that this lady would have had any motivation to take me out of the car. Knowing myself and my mechanical inclination and strength even as a child, I believe I had observed my father opening the door and figured out how to do it myself. I was likely impatient, opened the door, got out of the car, and went looking for him.

Whatever the case, the hand of God was protecting me yet again because I could easily have walked into the street. Once again, there were supernatural—or should I say, statistically improbable—interventions of protection. I absolutely believe the angel of the Lord does encamp round about the righteous to deliver them (Psalm 34:7). And angels protect us from dangers that we never even realize are present. God obviously has to make up for the carelessness of children, but even that carelessness is somewhat of an indication of trust. Children aren't worried about anything; they just live their lives with an expectation that somebody else is going to take care of them. In the same way, we are actually legal dependents of God, and He has obligated Himself to care for us. As much as it is a parent's job to take care of his child, it is God who cares even more, and receives the ultimate pleasure of caring for those who trust in Him. The trust of a child is a beautiful example of what God wants to accomplish in all of us. As adults, we must purposefully shed our independence and become childlike, putting all of our confidence in God.

Take heed that you do not despise one of these little
ones, for I say to you that in heaven their angels
always see the face of My Father who is in heaven.
Matthew 18:10

I Can't Stop Loving You

One of the most amusing stories my mother ever told me about myself happened when I was three years old. My mother was driving as I stood on the front seat next to her. These were the days before child car seats or seat belts were mandatory. Parents would often just put a hand over your chest to restrain you when braking, to keep you from falling forward.

My mom had the radio tuned to WRVA-AM radio in Richmond, which I remember as my parents' exclusive and favorite radio station. Ray Charles had released his song "I Can't Stop Loving You" one year earlier, and it was playing on the radio as we drove along. When the song reached the chorus, my mom said that, to her surprise and amazement, I began singing at the top of my lungs, "I can't stop loving you," in perfectly matched pitch.

She would always laugh when she told me that story. Little did she know that I had been listening and learning, and I surprised her with my first vocal performance!

As comical as I find this, I realize that the hand of God can be seen even in this. To think that God would use a song by Ray Charles to inspire me to sing! I guess I was like Moses, who was trained in all the wisdom of Egypt, and then God used his education and training for His glory. Ultimately, I would be called to music ministry, but God used secular music for my training.

Children are sponges. They absorb and assimilate information at an early age faster and more efficiently than they ever will at any other time in their lives. That is why it is so important to be careful how we speak and act in the presence of children. Everything that they see, hear, and feel affects them one way or another. For me in this instance, I was absorbing melody and lyrics that my mom couldn't imagine I would be able to replicate. So, I will have to say a big thank you to Mr. Ray Charles for being my first inspiration to sing.

Papa, My Maternal Grandfather

My maternal grandfather holds a special place in my heart. First of all, my name, William Harvey Gaines, is a combination of the first name of my paternal grandfather William and my maternal grandfather Harvey. My grandparents lived with us at one point, and there was something my grandfather said to me that, quite frankly, just went completely over my head at the time.

I was about five years old, and Papa was sitting in the living room rocking in his rocking chair and smoking his pipe, as usual. As I walked past him, he looked at me, took the pipe out of his mouth, and remarked, "Bill Boy," (that was what he called me), "I believe you are going to be a preacher." He put his pipe back into his mouth and didn't say another word.

I thought absolutely nothing of this statement at the time because the last thing I would ever think about at that age was being a preacher. I didn't know it then, but Papa would be the first person to ever speak to me what I would come to believe was a prophetic utterance concerning the call of God on my life.

There are two things I inherited from Papa. One is my love for music. Papa gave piano lessons and was also the choir director for several churches. The other is my love for fishing. Papa made me my first fishing pole from a small sapling he cut down for me and told me it was going to be my fishing pole. The only problem was that it had to dry out first. I probably wore Papa out asking if the pole was dry enough yet! It finally dried out, and he tested it by bending it. I remember him taking his pocketknife, cutting a notch, and tying some green braided fishing line around the groove. He put a cork and hook on the line, and I was delighted. I now had my first fishing pole, all rigged and ready to catch fish. My daddy had a compost pile in the backyard, and we dug nightcrawler worms out of it to use as our fishing bait.

I will never forget my first fishing trip. My brother Herman was driving, and we went fishing at the Chickahominy River off U.S. Route 1 in Richmond. I caught seven bluegills that day. When we got home, Papa taught me how to scale, gut, and clean the fish, and my mother cooked them. I wouldn't have imagined then that fishing would become one of the most serene, contemplative, and prayerful activities that I would enjoy. Those countless hours of peaceful prayer, thought, songwriting, and problem-solving while fishing have been some of the best hours of my life.

Children have special relationships with their grandparents. This became even more real to me when I became a grandparent myself. The mere fact that I can recount all these facts over sixty years later with such a feeling of gratitude is a great indicator of just how much grandparents have an effect on grandkids. Once again, it's that generational calling, declaration of faith, and ministry that was implanted in me by the words of my grandfather.

The Gorilla

I was about five years old when I was sitting next to my father one Sunday morning in church. The next thing I remembered was waking up in the hospital with EEG electrodes connected to my head. I had blacked out in church, and my parents had rushed me to the hospital. I can only surmise that I had some type of seizure. I never had another one of those episodes, but I do remember taking a prescription medication that consisted of red and white capsules. Shortly after that I began to have a horrible recurring nightmare that I was on a mountain and a gorilla would chase me to the end of a cliff. I would wake up in absolute terror. I would then go to my parents' bed, and they, in their mercy, would allow me to get in their bed to comfort me in my distress.

I don't know what those pills were for, but I do remember around that same time I started having migraine headaches. Those headaches would continue until I was fourteen. My cousin Dee asked me about my headaches one day, and I told him that they had mysteriously disappeared. He was delighted, and he told me he'd been praying that God would heal me of them. God did heal me of those migraine headaches, and I consider that another example of the healing hand of God in my life.

School Years

Richmond Public Schools: Seed Bed of Evangelism

In these present times, you would be hard-pressed to find anyone who would think public schools would be a place where they taught the gospel. But I experienced some events that showed the hand of God working even through the public school system. In June 1963, the Supreme Court handed down a ruling regarding the separation of church and state. I am so grateful to have had teachers who were defiant of that ruling. We still had prayer in our classes, and we learned and sang hymns also. It is so obvious to me that some of my earliest learning of doctrine came from hymns. Think about the lyrics to this familiar hymn:

Trust And Obey

When we walk with the Lord In the light of his word,
What a glory he sheds on our way,
As we do his goodwill, he abides with us still
And with all who will trust and obey
Trust and obey, for there's no other way
To be happy in Jesus but to trust and obey

Lead Me to Calvary

This wouldn't happen in a public school classroom today, but my second grade teacher, Mrs. Banks, taught the class a new song: "Lead Me to Calvary." I remember the day I learned it and came home to sing it for my mom. The delight she expressed hearing me sing that song was palpable. She immediately went over to the piano and started playing it as I sang along. My mom had an incredible ear; she could hear a song and then go straight to the piano and play it in any key. That is a skill I never quite perfected.

The most significant benefit of all of this was that I always had a thing for lyrics, and I always wanted to not only know the lyrics but what they meant. The tradition of my mom playing—and me singing—hymns became one of the most significant contributors to my understanding of Christian doctrine. I would later record the song "Lead Me to Calvary" on my *Ten Thousand Angels* CD, another evidence of the hand of God guiding me from my earliest years.

Lead Me to Calvary

King of my life, I crown thee now
Thine shall the glory be
Lest I forget Thy thorn-crowned brow
Lead me to Calvary
Lest I forget Gethsemane
Lest I forget thine agony
Lest I forget Thy love for me
Lead me to Calvary

Devil's Food Cake

Another layer of accountability I grew up with was my Aunt Betty. She was the head chef at our elementary school. You could say that we had family-style cooking every day for lunch. One of my many favorite lunch

16

desserts was devil's food cake, a rich, thick, moist chocolate cake with chocolate icing that I just loved.

I loved it so much that one day when the bell sounded for our lunch period to end and for us to head back to class, I stuffed the remainder of my cake into my mouth because I couldn't bear to leave any behind. As I tried to swallow, I felt the cake go down my windpipe.

I was horrified, and for the first time in my life I couldn't breathe in or out. I don't know where I got the idea, but I rushed to the bathroom, already beginning to tingle because of the amount of time that I could not breathe. I got into one of the stalls, stood over the toilet, and exhaled as hard as I could. The tube of cake shot out of my airway.

I could have choked to death that day. Once again, my life was preserved—the hand of God. I've had so many encounters that could have ended with the loss of my life that it almost seems unreal. Each of these events just simply makes me more grateful I am alive, even though I surely kept my angels busy!

Mrs. McClain, 1967

My seventh grade homeroom teacher, Mrs. McClain, was bold and defiant against the Madelyn Murray O'Hare ruling that eliminated prayer in public schools. Every morning she would pray over us before the school day started. Thank God for Christian teachers! I am the beneficiary of her belief in the power of prayer. I know with certainty that her prayers had a wonderful and positive effect on my life in the known and the unknown. She also set an example for me of the importance of putting God first by starting out the day in prayer. I'm forever grateful for that experience, and for learning the principle of giving God the first fruits of my day, a practice that is consistent in my life even now.

Confess your trespasses to one another, and pray for one another, that you may be healed. The effective, fervent prayer of a righteous man avails much.
James 5:16

Tell Uncle Herman on 'Em

When I was growing up, the Washington Park area of Richmond was like a village where everyone knew everyone, and you knew that if you were observed doing something wrong by an adult, your parents would hear about it. Aunt Betty, my maternal grandfather's sister, was the organist at St. John Baptist Church in Washington Park, where she was also the director of the youth choir.

I don't exactly know how my brother Jonathan and I were recruited to be a part of this choir, but there we were at the youth choir rehearsal. One day we were cutting up, and Aunt Betty turned to reprimand us for our behavior. My cousin Wanda chimed in with adult-like authority, advising, "Aunt Betty, all you have to do is tell Uncle Herman on 'em. He'll fix them."

That was a profoundly true statement! Telling my dad would definitely fix us! I laugh with great fondness every time I think back on that situation. Wanda's words would become a favorite quote that my brother Jonathan and I would rhythmically mimic and then break into laughter.

I thank God for the additional layer of accountability we grew up with. It taught us to respect authority and that the long arm of our parent's law extended through neighbors' eyes. We really are, or should be, subject to one another as far as inspiring each other to do good. But of course, the knowledge that there is a higher authority, like parents or uncles, is an additional incentive to do what's right!

Music as a Youth

Piano Lessons

I was about six years old when my maternal grandfather, Papa, attempted to give me piano lessons. I didn't last long, getting my fingers whacked with his pipe whenever I hit the wrong key. Besides all that, it seemed so dull compared to being outside playing. Oh, how I would wish later that I had been forced to take those piano lessons! But in the overall scheme of things, I'm grateful we always had a piano in our home.

The Recorder

In those days in Richmond Public Schools, everybody in the class got a little black flute called a recorder, along with a songbook. I can still remember how to play "Twinkle, Twinkle, Little Star" on the recorder, and that was the only song I ever played.

Musical Ear Testing

I think I was in the fourth grade when we went to the cafeteria to take a pitch perception test. All I remember about that day was that I panicked when the teacher played different notes up and down the piano keyboard and repeatedly asked, "Is this note lower or higher?" I failed the test and was not recommended to play a tonal instrument. So, I became a drummer, first on the bass drum and then on the snare drum.

Richmond Public Schools on Parade

I guess the one saving grace for me as a musician was the fact that I could sing. The gift of singing would lead to me being chosen to be part of a mass choir composed of Richmond Public Schools elementary school students. As a choir, we made a live recording at the Richmond Mosque. The title of the album was *Richmond Public Schools on Parade*. Some of the songs included were "Edelweiss" and "This is My Country." My mom and dad were so supportive; they said they could hear me singing even though I was amongst a choir of 300 voices. I guess that's just a parent thing!

"D Drummer"

I continued to play snare drum as part of the school band throughout elementary school, and when I went on to Chandler Junior High School, I chose the band as an elective. My band teacher was Janet Worsham, a trumpet player. I don't know exactly how I did it, but at the end of the seventh grade, my grade was a D. When I approached Ms. Worsham about my class and that I wanted to be in the band the next year, she replied, "I don't know if we can use a D drummer." Ouch.

The words stung like a bee but stirred up in me a desire to prove myself. Ms. Worsham gave me another chance, and I excelled, so much so that she chose me to join the orchestra. She gave me the assignment of playing the kettle drum (timpani) and along with this new assignment came tuning the timpani with a foot pedal. It was a significant boost to my confidence when I was allowed to play a tonal instrument.

That was one of the greatest lessons I learned about receiving correction. I may have had a rough start as a musician, but God had a plan for my life, and He would bring it to pass! I just had to cooperate with Him and walk into those plans.

A man's gift makes room for him, and puts him before great men.
Proverbs 18:16

If You Can't Hear, You Sure Can Feel

I don't remember the year, but it was summertime, sometime after 1963 because we had moved into the new home that my parents had built. My father had a brand-new chain-link fence installed around the property. This fence served two purposes: one, to keep danger out, and secondly and more importantly, to keep us in. With both of my parents working, this was their perfect remedy to keep us safe and out of trouble while they were at work.

So, the commandment was handed down: "Do Not Go Out Of This Yard." Well, you can imagine what happened. I didn't go far at all, just outside of the gate, and while I was standing there, I looked up and there at the corner of Corbin and Akron Street was my mother stepping off the Greater Richmond Transit Company bus. I knew there was no need in trying to duck back into the yard because my mother had already seen me standing outside the gate. I guess I figured that if I acted like I didn't think I was doing anything wrong, maybe this pretense would earn me some consideration or mercy. So I just stood there as she walked the block and a half, making her way home. When she arrived, she greeted me with the sweetest, calmest voice and said, "Hi Billy, how are you?" I breathed a sigh of relief, thinking I had escaped the consequences of my disobedience. As she opened the gate and walked up the sidewalk toward the stoop to our side door, I felt all the more certain that I was not going to receive any kind of reprimand at all. When we got into the house, she turned to me, and in that same calm, sweet voice, she said, "Now, didn't I tell you not to go out of this yard?"

I heard a saying once that "vengeance is best served cold." Well, my mom was now serving it up sweet. My mouth dropped open in speechless shock, and I remember thinking to myself, "Wait, I thought I got away with this." I knew that when she instructed me to go to my room, it was not for me to take a nap, and time-outs had not even been invented yet. My bedroom would now be where one of the most effective lessons about obedience and second-guessing the instructions of my mother would be emblazoned on my back side. The scripture she always quoted, "obedience is better than sacrifice," took on new meaning. My sister Barbara reminded me a few years ago that one of my mother's sayings was, "If you can't hear, you sure can feel." I didn't listen, but I sure did feel the loving and disciplining hand of God through my mother!

Summer of 1968

The year 1968 was, without a doubt, the most tumultuous year that I can ever remember. The only thing that came close was that twenty-second day of November 1963, when I stood outside our home and watched as kids in the distance were practically racing down Akron Street away from Mary M. Scott Elementary School. As they neared, I could see tears in their eyes. Among them was my older sister Barbara. I never will forget how she declared through her tears that President John F. Kennedy was dead.

The year 1968 would bear the same sadness in multiples: on April 4, Martin Luther King Jr. was assassinated in Memphis, Tennessee, and on June 6, Robert "Bobby" Kennedy was assassinated in Los Angeles, California. But that year would also carry one of the most exceptionally pivotal occurrences in my life.

I was thirteen years old, and it was Friday, June 21, just fifteen days after Robert Kennedy's assassination. I had just come home from the playground when, for reasons I still can't understand, I decided to sneak out of the house while my parents were distracted. I went one block over on Cheatwood Avenue to my older brother Herman Jr.'s home and took my nephew Herman III (KeKe's) bicycle for a ride.

I rode back down to the playground, which was pitch dark by this time, and then decided to rush home, fearing that my mother would discover my absence. I exited the schoolyard playground at Mary M. Scott Elementary School, pedaling as fast as I could down Akron Street. When I approached the intersection of Akron and Moss Side Avenue, I noticed car headlights coming from the right, but I was sure I could beat the car across the intersection. Instead, I met the car in the middle of the intersection. I remember the collision and how the headlights of that car illuminated the right side of the bicycle. I felt the impact and remember being airborne and spinning in the air, but I have no recollection at all of hitting the ground.

In those days in my neighborhood, people sat on their front porches and talked at night. The account the neighbors gave was that the collision with the car had thrown me as high as the power lines. They would later tell my parents they had uttered, "We know that child is dead."

They ran over to where I had landed, and to their amazement, I jumped up and started running. The neighbors caught me and laid me down on the ground. I had a bleeding wound on the right side of my head, which they wrapped with a towel, pinning me down on the ground so I wouldn't move. I remember from this point on feeling the pressure of being held down on the ground, and then feeling what seemed to be a tingle on the right side of my head. I slipped my right hand under the towel wrapped around my head, and as my fingers sank into a gouged, bloody head wound, I screamed in terror. Shortly after that, I heard my dad's anguished voice asking, "Who hit him? Who hit him?"

Immediately I said, "Daddy, don't do anything to that man; it was my fault." The next thing I felt was Daddy's tear-drenched face pressed against mine. Out of nowhere, I uttered the words, "Daddy, I'm gonna pray real hard."

It would be years later before I drew the correlation between the tears of my grandfather falling into my daddy's face, and tears of my daddy falling into my face.

I was transported to the hospital by ambulance, examined, and X-rayed from head to toe. I had no broken bones or internal injuries. The severe gouging of my head wound precluded the use of stitches to close it. They could only pack it with gauze, apply the antibacterial salve, give me a turban wrap for my head, and send me home.

It was a miracle I lived through this. This close brush with death was the turning point in my life and a realization of my mortality. It was this near-death situation that let me know God had spared my life for a purpose. Though I had been in church all my life and had been baptized at age six, I was entering my teen years without a relationship with Christ. But more miracles were coming my way. Later that year, my cousin Thomas Todd (Dee) would come visit Richmond from Hampton, Virginia, entirely on fire for Jesus, and his witness for Christ and the message of repentance from sin would lead to me giving my life fully to Christ.

When I was young, my mother told me that if I believed in Jesus, that after resurrection, I would live forever and never die. I believed that so much that I actually went around the street to my brother's house and started preaching the same message to my peers. I may not have been living fully for Jesus, but

I did believe what my mother told me about Him. By preaching that to my peers I was already beginning to fulfill what my Papa had said to me: "Bill Boy, I believe you're going to be a preacher." When my cousin came to town, he began to disciple me and start the process of sanctification in my life.

Lingle Hall

The summer of 1969 was particularly fun. We would walk over two miles from home to Richmond's Battery Park swimming pool to swim. Then we would walk a mile and a half to Lingle Hall on Brook Road to roller skate in the basement of the building. There was a home in that area where the homeowner would allow us to swim in their private pool. After that, we would head home and have an enormous lunch.

One day while skating in the basement of Lingle Hall, I was playing with my nephew KeKe, chasing him around the skating rink with my hands stretched out in front of me like the Frankenstein monster. As I approached him, he ducked suddenly, and I went off to the side of the rink where there were wooden folding chairs. I put my hands out to break my fall, and my right hand went through the middle of the folding chair. Suddenly, the chair folded and closed, with my fingers flat against the back of the chair and my palm flat against the seat of the chair. Three of my fingers broke the vertical boards out of the back of the chair. My pinky finger was dislocated and pushed up over the knuckle. It was the weirdest sight to see my little finger perpendicular to the back of my hand.

Richmond Memorial Hospital was then located right behind Lingle Hall, and my mother came from work and took me to the emergency room. The doctor injected the base of my finger with Novocain and attempted to reset my finger, but he couldn't do it. My mother had to take me to a bone specialist in Richmond's Southside. He sedated me, so I don't know how he got my finger back in place, but when I woke up, I had a cast on my arm with an aluminum splint protruding out of the hand end of the cast and my little finger taped to the brace.

That ended my snare drum playing for the time being, and I didn't have any musical involvement at John Marshall High School at all, other than drumming on the desk in one of my classes and singing gospel songs with my buddy Larry Miles. Interestingly enough, Larry Miles would eventually become a pastor at Church of God in Christ in Richmond.

Sometimes in life there are setbacks. We don't always know why they happen in the moment, but in the course of time, they actually turn into a redirection of our path.

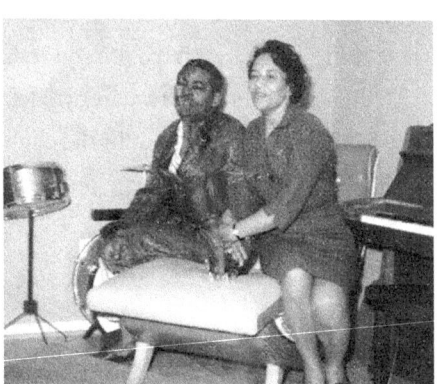

My Mom and Dad.

Walking with Jesus

———•◆•———

There's Room at the Cross for You

I remember so vividly the day that it was fully settled in my heart that I was saved. I was fourteen years old. Music, as you already know, had always played a big part in my home, and some of my musical taste was shaped by my mother's choices. Actually, some of my fondest and earliest memories were of Christmas music. The first Christmas album that I remember was *The Perry Como Christmas Album*, then Bing Crosby's *White Christmas*, and finally, my favorite of all time, *The Nat King Cole Christmas Album*. Interestingly, I would find a few decades later that *The Nat King Cole Christmas Album* was produced by Ralph Carmichael, the founder and owner of Light Records, which is the label that brought us Andraé Crouch and the Winans.

But the greatest and most profound album in my life was that of Kate Smith. She recorded an album of hymns entitled *Just a Closer Walk with Thee* which contained the song "Room at the Cross for You." I remember so distinctly lying on a couch in our den as this album was playing. In that moment, as "Room at the Cross for You" played on the stereo, it was as if there was a convergence of everything that I had ever heard of or had been taught about Jesus Christ. Not only did the information make sense, but I knew in my heart that all of those wonderful promises of God were for me. Another song on that same album was "Ten Thousand Angels." In 2005, I included both of those songs on a record, even making "Ten Thousand Angels" the title track on my album. At fourteen I was just a boy listening to music, but in the plan, foreknowledge, and purposeful hand of God, I was a planted seed that would grow and bear fruit for the kingdom of God.

The Cross and the Switchblade

The year was 1970, and I was in my freshman year at John Marshall High School. My ninth-grade English teacher was a lady by the name of Ola Dandridge. Ms. Dandridge took our class on a field trip to see a movie at the Willow Lawn Theatre in Richmond's West End. I had no idea what I was in for or how this field trip would impact my life.

The film we went to see that day was *The Cross and the Switchblade*, starring Pat Boone as David Wilkerson and Erik Estrada as Nicky Cruz. All I can say is that as I watched that movie, my heart just burned inside of me. I felt so grateful to know the Jesus who was glorified in this movie, and my faith, courage, and boldness for Christ were greatly increased.

In 1973, my eleventh-grade social studies teacher had what I would have to characterize as a study of religion week. She invited speakers from numerous different religions to come to our classroom and talk to the students about their faith.

I distinctly remember there was a Catholic priest, someone from the Baha'i religion, and a Muslim. On Friday, the last day of the religion study week, a man from New York by the name of Victor Torres came to speak to us. As he began to tell his story, the first thing I noticed was the stark contrast between the philosophy of all the other former speakers and the power of God I sensed as he began to pour out clear evidence of the hand of God in his life. He had been delivered from drug addiction and a life of unthinkable crime. As he continued to speak, he revealed he had come to the Lord through Nicky Cruz, the man portrayed in the movie *The Cross and the Switchblade.*

I was shocked. How could it be that my ninth-grade teacher had taken our class on a field trip to see a movie about David Wilkerson and Nicky Cruz, and now, here in my eleventh-grade classroom, was a real, live disciple of Nicky Cruz's ministry, standing there ministering under the power of God! This encounter greatly emboldened me and spurred me on with more determination than ever to serve God with all my heart.

Twenty years later in 1990, while ministering in song at Richmond Christian Center, I looked out in the congregation and saw Ms. Ola Dandridge sitting on the front row. When I approached her, she didn't even remember me, but I told her that she had a great impact on my Christian life by taking us to see *The Cross and the Switchblade.*

It's amazing to me the number of public school teachers who played a role in my Christian life. Once again, it indicates the amazing situations and people God will use to accomplish His purpose in us. I take great comfort that, even as I go forward in life now, I can know that He's the same God who has always protected me, who has directed my steps, and He is not through with me. He is the same yesterday, today, and forever.

The Jesus Movement

I am a product of the Jesus Movement. When my cousin Dee moved from Hampton, Virginia, to Richmond to attend Virginia Commonwealth University, he introduced me to The Open Doorway Coffeehouse. It was located on Grace Street in the Fan District of Richmond, right next door to the Biograph Movie Theater. It was modeled after David Wilkerson's coffeehouse in New York City. Rich and April Blue, the founders, had traveled to New York City to study and be trained in coffeehouse ministry under David Wilkerson. The bottom floor was a bookstore and meeting place, and the upper floors were apartments. Though it wasn't a commune, the building did have a number of Christians living there, including my cousin. The atmosphere was one of peace and love. I remember that there were multiple fluorescent posters of Jesus on the walls, including one of the most prominent images of that time, that of Jesus pointing up, with the words "One Way."

Open Doorway Coffehouse circa 1974. Cousin Dee in bottom left corner.

Me singing and playing piano at Open Doorway Coffeehouse
after the move to Broad Street in 1977.

I say that I am a product of the Jesus Movement because it was my first exposure to what I would characterize as simple, organic Christianity. It had none of the elements that I would find on Sunday morning at St. John United Holy Church: the choir, the organ, shouting (dancing), the building, and the climactic sermon. Instead of people wearing suits, ties, and hats, the people at the coffeehouse were mostly hippies in blue jeans who were unchurched but loved Jesus with all their hearts. The music was primarily acoustic guitar and vocal-driven. I remember one of the most prominent songs was "I Wish We'd All Been Ready" by Randy Stonehill. My most memorable friends there were Rich and April Blue, Brian and Audrey Hingley, and Willy and Linda Kaffenburger. For me, it became a sanctuary. I would even go there and pray during the week sometimes. It was there that I learned to seek God's face and to hear His voice. It was also a place of solidification of God's call on my life for ministry.

Repentance

I was only fifteen years old and a baby Christian when I thought I'd fallen in love with a girl I met at Chandler Junior High School. I now know I was only infatuated with her. Before that year, she always seemed to be out of my league and out of my reach, but for whatever reason, we now had converged in mutual attraction and a puppy love relationship. So, the insanity of tying up the telephone line to talk about absolutely nothing had begun, and the amount of time I was dedicating to this new-found relationship was now evident and

Brian and Audrey Hingley wedding. I am in the background wearing white pants and multi-colored dashiki.

concerning to those who were closest to me. Those who genuinely love and care for you will challenge you, but especially those who watch out for your soul. My cousin Dee was one of those people, and he very directly told me he believed my relationship with my girlfriend was drawing me away from the Lord, and he was right. My mother also noticed my drifting, and she shocked me with bold and direct questioning that had me saying to myself, "I can't believe she just asked me that." But because I knew they loved me, their concern helped to deepen and intensify the conviction of the Holy Spirit in my life.

Surprisingly, the catalyst for me completely breaking free of the relationship came from a source I couldn't have imagined. Audrey and Brian Hingley were one of the couples I had met at the Open Doorway Coffeehouse through my cousin Dee. He also sang at their wedding, which I attended. It was the first "born-again Christian" wedding I had ever attended, and that couple became the inspiration for my dream of

Brian and Audrey Hingley wedding. My cousin Dee is in white beside the bride.

marrying a born-again Christian woman. I don't even remember how all of this came about, but my cousin Dee and I ended up riding with Audrey and Brian to Virginia Beach to attend a church service at Rock Church. I don't remember who the speaker was, or even any of the details of that church service. What I remember the most about that trip was that as we were traveling on I-64 East near the Hampton Coliseum, we were driving through a construction zone with the orange and white construction barrels on the side of the road. The car ahead of us hit a deer, the deer was thrown up into the air, and was flipping end over end before crashing back down to the ground. This was the first time I had ever witnessed anything like this, and I felt so sorry for the deer. What no one else riding in that car knew, though, was the intense fear and conviction I felt about my present situation, and the inescapable feeling that the death of this deer was in some way a warning to me. God used that situation to bring me to a place of repentance and rededication of myself to Him.

Piano Player

I was now seventeen years old. I had been praying and asking God to show me His will for my life, and I had a deep sense that I was supposed to be involved in music. Almost out of nowhere, I had a desire to learn to play piano. I asked my sister Barbara to teach me scales on the piano, and I just took off teaching myself to play. I had been learning to play all of one week when on a Saturday night at the Open Doorway Coffeehouse, April Blue spoke up and asked if there was anybody who had a song they would like to share. Instantly I heard in my spirit, "Don't be afraid. Give what you have, and I will bless you." I got up, went to the piano, and for the first time sang and played publicly. That was a pivotal moment for me as I yielded to the hand of God. I had every intention of becoming a mechanical engineer and an inventor, but God had a different plan. So, when I went out and bought a 73-key Fender Rhodes Suitcase Electric Piano and said that I was going to be a musician, my father was baffled, to say the least. I hadn't been involved in music at all in high school, and now here I was applying for admission to Virginia Commonwealth University to be a music composition and theory major. Miraculously, after four years of not even touching a snare drum, I sight-read the audition on snare drum and was accepted directly into the Music Department. Clearly, that was the hand of God guiding my future!

Beanie and the Summer of 1971

I look back on the summer of 1971 with great fondness for several reasons, but especially because of the spiritual lessons I learned. My Uncle Ellis Bates Sr., the husband of my mother's sister Lucy, worked at the Baughman Printing Company in Richmond. That summer he got my cousin Dee and me hired for summer jobs there. My mother's brother Joseph (Uncle Joe) worked there, also. I worked in the shipping department binding pallets of boxes and loading them onto trucks with a pallet jack. As you can imagine, a shipping dock with a lot of guys working will inevitably turn into an environment of a lot of talk, both good and bad. This shipping dock was no exception, and nothing makes you stand out as a Christian more than when you exhibit an unexpected response to some off-color statement, or your answer to the question, "Ain't that right, man?" is, "Well, I'm a Christian, and I don't do that."

Trying to witness to these guys about Christ was no easy task. One day, after a pretty good lashing from them, one of them looked me straight in the face and said, "People like you belong in Westbrook." Westbrook was the psychiatric hospital in Richmond. Later on, I was sitting inside the loading dock office eating my lunch when one of the guys named Beanie came in. He saw me eating, and said, "Man, I forgot my lunch." I immediately gave him one of my sandwiches, and he broke down and started crying.

Now keep in mind, this is a guy about eighteen years old. I was completely shocked. He began to explain that he knew all of the things we were saying about Jesus were true because his grandmother had taught him those things all his life. He said he just didn't want to get teased along with us. I invited Beanie to come to the coffeehouse, and he did. We talked and prayed, and he committed his life to Christ. Then he took his pack of cigarettes out of his back pocket and threw them on the floor. A while later I found out from a friend of mine that Beanie was living in Texas and was a preacher.

Prayers of 1972

It was in 1972 that I really began to develop a prayer life. Early on as a young Christian, I remember very distinctly that my cousin Dee, my cousin Charles Johnson, and my brother Jonathan would have prayer meetings at night over at John Marshall High School. I decided to join them. There were several marble benches that lined the rear entry, and it was a relatively short, paved drive leading up to the back of the school. We would call out the names of every one of our family members, praying for them, and we began to see an amazing revival in our family. I would also go and pray regularly at the coffeehouse. There was just something about that environment that inspired me. Without anyone really teaching me, I understood from the Word of God and from experience that Jesus loved me and that He did want me to have my heart's desire. From the simplest prayer of forgetting to bring a pencil to class, praying for one, and finding one in my desk, to praying for friends and relatives and seeing them come to Christ, to seeing a car on the car lot that I wanted, asking for it, and receiving it, or praying for a piano and having my prayers answered, showed me that God heard and answered my prayers. I would see hundreds, if not thousands, of prayers answered through the years. I developed a lifestyle of prayer and seeking God early on and have kept that through my life.

February of 1974

The day was Thursday, February 21, 1974. This day still has special significance to me because my mother wrote, in freshly poured concrete in front of our home, "February 21, 1974. Billy's 18th Birthday." The Richmond redevelopment project was in full swing, and for the first time we would have concrete sidewalks and asphalt streets. Another memorable thing about that day was the construction workers who were helping in the redevelopment program were seated at our dinner table during their lunch break. My mother and father had both been laid off from the Jefferson Manufacturing Company. When the redevelopment project began, my mother saw a money-making possibility. She came up with the idea of offering home-cooked meals at a dinner table to the workers, accommodating five at a time. As you can imagine, this was a big hit with the workers. I would later learn from my brother Jonathan that my mother was grossing $500 per week with her home-cooked lunch service.

This was one of the greatest lessons I learned about how God will provide for you in hard times, but also of how to think creatively to generate unconventional sources of income. I'm also grateful for the work ethic that I learned from my parents. Saturdays were always workdays at our home, and we knew that we would not be doing any kind of playing until we had completed our assigned chores. Some Saturdays, that work portion was extended; after cutting the grass at home, my father would take us across town to Churchill to cut the grass for our Aunt Florence, my dad's sister. From that grew my brother Jonathan's and my first entrepreneurial venture. We decided to start cutting lawns for money. We approached my dad about our idea, and he told us that he didn't want us to use his lawn mower for that. He would buy us a lawn mower, and then let us pay him for it out of our earnings. In no time, we were able to pay Dad back for his investment, and the rest was profit for us.

One of my parents' financial mentors was a lady named Katie Carpenter, a Jewish woman who lived in the Ginter Park area of Richmond. Mrs. Carpenter really loved my mother, so much so that she included my mother in her will. My father had approached her for a loan to buy a car. She told him, "Herman, don't buy a new car. Buy a home." Mrs. Carpenter loaned my parents money for their first home. She was one of the people God put in my parents' lives to help set them up for success, and my siblings and I were also the beneficiaries of those blessings.

Falling in Love

$\bullet\!\!\blacklozenge\!\!\bullet$

The Spring of 1974

I would have to consider the spring of 1974 as one of the happiest times of my life. I had great expectation for the future, and I was growing in my musical abilities. I was working full time at Medical College of Virginia because I only needed to attend half a day in my senior year at John Marshall High School in order to graduate. My cousin Cheryl Todd had also moved to Richmond to attend VCU along with her brother Dee. Cheryl was dating a guy named Shell Thomas, who was the choir director at their home church, St. John Church of God in Christ. His younger sister Boose was in the choir, and Cheryl had brought a cassette tape of Boose singing "By the Time I Get To Heaven." I heard it and loved her voice, and I quipped, "She sounds so cute, I want to squeeze her."

I knew in advance that Shell and Cheryl were driving up from Hampton to Richmond on a Friday night because Dee and Cheryl were singing the next day for Willie and Linda Kaffenberger's wedding. They were friends from the coffeehouse. I was anxiously awaiting Shell and Cheryl's arrival at my cousin Wanda Falden's house. When the doorbell rang, I ran to answer it. Peering out through the peep hole, I saw a distorted, fish-eye view of a face I didn't recognize. As I opened the door, in walked one of the cutest girls I had ever seen in my life. My cousin Cheryl put her hands on the girl's shoulders and said, "This is the girl you said you wanted to squeeze." It was Sarah Bernice Thomas (Boose). I was truly stricken, both with attraction and embarrassment! I knew they were all going back to Hampton Sunday night, so I made up my mind right then and there that either I was going to make a complete fool of myself or I was going to win this girl's heart.

Every chance I got, I sought some kind of interaction with her, even if it was only a glance. In retrospect, Sarah probably thought, "This crazy boy is staring me down!" But as time moved on that weekend, one of the things she wanted was to hear me sing because my cousin Cheryl had talked so much about it.

We were on the second floor of the Open Doorway Coffeehouse, and I found myself in the kitchen with her. She pleaded with me to sing a song. So, I finally gave in and sang Donny Hathaway's version of the song "For All We Know." I think that song may have affected her.

For All We Know

> For all we know we may never meet again
> Before you go, make this moment sweet again
> We won't say goodnight until the last moment
> I'll hold up my hand and my heart will be in it

As the weekend went on, we—and by we, I mean my cousin Cheryl and I, Sarah, her brother Shell, and their sister Olease—would go over to Bryan Park. While I was seated next to Sarah, she rested her elbow on my leg, and as silly as it seems, in my puppy love estimation of things, this was a sure sign that

Sarah and me at the sea wall in Fort Monroe, Virginia.

she kind of liked me. Further evidence to my adolescent brain that she was interested in me was that while descending some stairs at Bryan Park, she put her hands on my shoulders. By the time Sarah and her brother and sister climbed into the car that Sunday night to head back to Hampton, both of our hearts were connected.

Cause for Concern

It was my senior year in high school, and in my mind, a time when I had a clear understanding of God's purpose for my life. I heard a quote once that said, "The older I get, the smarter my father becomes." I've learned as a father myself that there are things children get involved in that become "cause for concern." In the father's mind, it is a matter of wanting to protect his children from harm and an attempt to launch them on a successful trajectory through life, but from the child's vantage point, it feels like the father is being controlling and fearful. Such was the case at this point in my relationship with my father.

Looking back, I can understand his fears and his logic. Let's face it, here I was, the son of a Baptist deacon, now spending my Friday and Saturday nights at a charismatic coffeehouse next to the Biograph Theater in the Fan District of Richmond, with what he would have considered to be White hippies in this new Jesus Movement. He was also concerned that I wasn't spending my time dating. Instead, I was "following behind Tom," his reference to my cousin Thomas (whom I called Dee). He expressed his dissatisfaction with this scenario and told me that if he knew I would be riding Tom around in my car instead of girls, he wouldn't have signed the loan for it. Add to that my purchase of a $900 Fender Rhodes Electric Piano only months after I had first started learning to play piano, and I am quite sure it seemed like erratic behavior.

What really frustrated him, though, was after high school when I told him I was dropping out of VCU to pursue music, and my subsequent move to Hampton. That just seemed to drive a wedge between us. All of this would be further exacerbated by the fact that I was part of a church plant in Richmond that didn't end well. The heartache that came out of that church plant was some of the worst pain I have ever felt, and that alone could be another book all by itself.

Yet in all of the dissension, I still see that the hand of God was at work in my life. It taught me I can't place my trust in people, and that even when leaders do fail, that is not an indication of the veracity or validity of the scripture or its principles. Just like our American Constitution is a benchmark for all of our laws, justice, and our very existence, so the Bible is our spiritual "constitution." When there are issues and disagreements, they should be settled by God's Word.

KeKe, 1974

My nephew Herman S. Gaines III (KeKe) was the son of my older brother. KeKe was more like a cousin than a nephew, since my brother Herman was twenty years older than me. The date was Friday, August 16, 1974. I was eighteen at the time and KeKe was fifteen. I had made a trip to Giant Food Store that morning in the West End of Richmond. On the way back home, I was pulled over by a Henrico County policeman, who took a tape measure and measured the distance between the bottom of my rear bumper and the ground and gave me a citation for my vehicle being jacked up too high. He also looked under my car and noticed the high-performance muffler and included that violation on the citation. I headed home to replace the muffler and to let air out of my adjustable shock absorbers.

I decided to change the muffler in the vacant lot next to my brother Herman's home. KeKe noticed me getting ready to change the muffler and insisted I let him do it. He was mechanically inclined and did an excellent job. As a reward, I took him to Bryan Park and allowed him to drive my car. The joy on his face is emblazoned on my mind. Later that night I headed out of town to Hampton for a weekend visit. It was Sunday morning at about 3:30 when the phone awakened me as I was sleeping on the floor of my Aunt Harriett's (my mother's sister) living room floor. There was the greatest sense of fear and dread that I had ever felt in my life in the ring of that phone. I just knew there was something terribly wrong. My cousin Cheryl answered the phone and told me that the call was for me. It was my mother. Even more dread gripped me now. I took the phone, and my mother told me that KeKe had drowned. I would later find out he had been out fishing with his family. His mother became distressed in the water next to the shipping dock at the post office in Yorktown, and in an attempt to save her, KeKe had jumped off the end of the dock and was swept away by the current. His body would be found three days later, a few miles from that location in the York River.

I was shocked. I knew personally that KeKe was an excellent swimmer from our frequent trips to the Battery Park swimming pool. How could this be? I collapsed into my cousin Cheryl's lap and hugged her and sobbed uncontrollably. I was devastated. I drove back to Richmond later that morning, and my cousin Wilbert rode with me just so I wouldn't be alone for the trip. When I arrived, the display of grief was like nothing I had ever seen from my family. I made it back to my bedroom, and there I saw KeKe's church clothes hanging over my bedroom door and his shoes at the base of the door. He was spending the night and was planning to go with my parents to church that Sunday morning. I buried my face into those clothes and drenched them with my tears. I would learn from my sister Barbara that KeKe had drawn a tub of water for his bath that night. He hadn't wanted to go fishing that night but was prodded into going. When Barbara arrived at my mom and dad's house, she saw the water for his intended bath still in the bathtub.

I very dreadfully headed to my brother Herman's house on the next street over. I walked down the alley and cut through a neighbor's yard. Heading towards me was my cousin Wanda Falden. I collapsed on her, weeping, and she told me later she felt that she was holding my whole weight. I would say that physically and spiritually at that moment, she was

43

bearing my grief. I finally made it to my brother Herman's house, and I found him in the back yard, sitting on the ground in the dust. He looked up at me and said, "I didn't mean to let him drown." One of the saddest things about that moment was that he felt he needed to apologetically explain the death of his precious and adored son was an accident. That image has stuck in my mind all these years. His sitting in the dust on the ground was the closest thing I have ever seen to what I would imagine Job looked like. This was the most devastating thing I had ever encountered, and his tragedy drove home a very real understanding of the uncertainty of life. Yet, despite that, it only proved to make me even more resolved to dedicate myself to the spreading of the gospel of Jesus Christ. It also gave me an even greater sense of the urgency of that Great Commission.

One other event that has remained an intriguing mystery to me, though, is the account of my nephew Mark Johnson of that fishing trip on that fateful morning. Fishing in the early morning was common in the area because some of the best fishing in the tidewater of Virginia was at night, in conjunction with the incoming or outgoing tide. Mark said that as they entered the area of the park near the York River, a Virginia state trooper appeared out of nowhere and detained the party of cars traveling together. The officer said the park was closed and though it was not illegal for them to go into the area, it was dangerous, and he recommended they not go into the area. Mark said that he stared intently at the officer because there was something surreal about him. As they continued their trek towards the park, Mark turned around and stared at the officer, and in his words, "I couldn't take my eyes off of him." As he stared at the officer, instead of fading from view with the increasing distance, he vanished instantly. I believe that this was an angel sent by God to warn them all, and a lesson about the importance of listening to the Holy Spirit when He speaks.

I-64 West

One Sunday night I was in the left lane of I-64 West, heading back to Richmond from Hampton. I don't even remember feeling sleepy, but I suddenly woke up and saw that I was headed straight for the left concrete rail on a bridge. I didn't have time to think. I turned my steering wheel ever so slightly to the right and just barely missed colliding with that rail, which would have meant certain death. I had a strong, tingling sensation from head to toe, and I was terrified and grateful all at the same time. Once again, I knew that my life had been saved by the hand of God.

Marty Dickerson, May of 1975

While in Richmond I had been going to school full time and working at MCV and UPS. When I moved to Hampton in 1975, I was able to transfer from the Richmond UPS hub to the Hampton hub. Shortly after that, I found an even better job at Howmet Turbine Components Corporation. This was truly designed by the hand of God because I would meet a guy named Marty Dickerson there. We worked together in the wax injection molding. He would be the greatest influence in my life as it relates to having a friend who was absolutely, completely sold out to God. I was truly fortunate to know this brother, and our daily fellowship as we worked together is still foundational in my Christian walk. I realized that God had brought me to Hampton and this place, and it was way more about building character in me than having a job or being in ministry.

Living Sacrifice

It was June of 1975 that I finally settled down in Hampton. All I knew was that I had a call of God on my life to pursue music ministry and that God had given me a "fitting help" in the person of Sarah Bernice Thomas. She was the namesake of her mother, who in her own right was a pianist and singer who played and sang at numerous churches in the Tidewater area. Shortly after I moved to Hampton, my cousin Charles Johnson moved to nearby Newport News. He was a drummer who had just finished his degree in music education at Shaw University in Raleigh, North Carolina. We became roommates and also bandmates. Our group was called Living Sacrifice.

Back row: me, Bill Smalt, Charles Johnson
Front row: Mike Ballard, Sarah, Kenneth Martin

Mike Ballard-bass, Bill Smalt-guitar, Charles Johnson-drums,
Kenneth Martin-congas. Sarah and I in front. Circa 1978

Sarah and I sang lead and harmony, and I also played keyboards. The rest of
the band included Mike Ballard on bass, Bill Smalt on guitar, Kenny Martin
on congas, Kevin Diggs on guitar, and Vivian Creekmore on flute.

Dating

Dating for Sarah and me would
eventually consist of Friday night and
Saturday rehearsals with the band,
Sunday morning and evening church
services, Wednesday night church
services, monthly Friday all-night
prayer meetings, and monthly prayer
breakfasts. Elder Doug Cornish was
the manager for our band and also a
chaperone for our engagements. That

was pretty much it for our time together, which resulted in a lot of solitude for me, but in the overall scheme of things, it worked out for our good. We had very little opportunity to focus on anything other than practicing and going to church together, which made it easier to endure all the tension and attraction that goes along with two young people falling in love.

Discouraged

I had moved to Hampton with only a few items: my Fender Rhodes piano and a mattress. Initially I stayed at my Aunt Harriet's home, but not long after that I got an apartment and ended up with a television, a kitchen table, and the stereo from my mom and dad's house. This was the first time I had lived on my own, and it quickly turned into the loneliest time I had ever experienced. In my mind, with the call of ministry that I had on my life, I figured I would be in full-time ministry in no time. Was I ever wrong.

I remember one day practicing on my piano and feeling so discouraged that I felt like tossing it out of the window. I turned off the piano and just sat on the floor in utter frustration. I got up, turned on the television, and immediately there was a minister talking about not wasting the gifts and talents God has given you. I remember specifically that he mentioned if you have an old clarinet that's been sitting in a closet, go get it and dust it off and use your talent for the Lord. I was shocked! I knew this was no coincidence, but that God was speaking to me through this minister on television.

Another thing that was a great encouragement to me was a dream I had one night. I dreamed I had walked into the living room of my apartment, and as I stood in front of the stereo, I heard my voice singing out of it. Now keep in mind, when I say stereo, I mean a stereo console that was actually a big piece of furniture. It was that same stereo that had been in our home in Richmond. It was the same stereo that I had spent countless hours listening to, studying my favorite singers. It was also the same stereo that I was listening to when I heard Kate Smith's version of "Room at The Cross for You" and committed my life to Christ.

Although I never heard myself sing through that particular stereo, that dream proved to be prophetic almost ten years later.

Vision in the Night

There are some things that happen to us that are so dramatic, they leave a permanent imprint on us. These are the things that we need only experience one time to know with absolute certainty that God does exist and that He is perpetually interacting with mankind. I have had only one distinct vision in my life, and I don't need another one to convince me of the presence and power of God. The year was 1976. I had moved out of my first apartment in Hampton to a new one. My bed was against the wall near a window. While I was sleeping, I saw a hand begin to descend from the sky. It grew closer and closer, and just as this hand was about to touch my face, I was awakened. I was terrified, and my heart was pounding. Immediately I heard the window next to my bed slide open, and cold air from the outside rush in. I was so frozen in fear, it was as if my body was immobilized. All I could do was say, "Hey!" I then heard the footsteps of whoever it was running away. I don't know what the intention of that person was, but I know I was awakened by the hand of God to prevent it.

Burglary

As the group Living Sacrifice progressed in ministry appearances, we were also able to acquire a new PA system. All the band's instruments and equipment were in the living room of my apartment where we routinely rehearsed. One night, while I was sleeping, I suddenly sat up in bed and was prompted to go into the living room. As I looked around the corner, there was a man with the PA system mixer board heading out the door. I yelled, "Hey!" and he fled. I followed him outside and found the mixing board lying in mud on the side of the building. I'm not sure how this guy got into the apartment. All I could think was that the door had been left unlocked by mistake. Here again, I am sure the Lord woke me up just in time to thwart this burglary attempt, but not soon enough for me to encounter the perpetrator inside of the apartment, which may have had dire consequences. Eventually, we moved all our equipment to our home church, and we would practice there instead of my apartment. Unfortunately, burglars broke into the church and stole the PA board and a guitar, but the church's insurance policy covered the theft, and we ended up with brand-new equipment that was superior to what was stolen.

Me with my niece Kathy Carey (left) and Sarah
(right) at the Open Doorway Coffeehouse, 1977.

My niece Kathy Carey (left), me, and Sarah, 1977.

New Doors Opening

The Summer of 1977

Our group, Living Sacrifice, had grown in popularity, and we had become regulars at places like Rock Church in Virginia Beach, Hampton Institute (now Hampton University), and the Fire Escape Coffeehouse in Virginia Beach. One of the elders of our church, Doug Cornish, was our manager and the director of Fellowship of Christian Athletes on

the Hampton Institute campus. He was also an enlisted member of the Air Force at Langley Air Force Base. Danniebelle Hall was a former member of the gospel group Andraé Crouch and the Disciples. She had recently gone solo and had released her first album on Light Records. It had quickly become one of my favorite albums, and Living Sacrifice performed the songs "Work the Works" and "He Giveth More Grace." So when Doug Cornish had

the idea of having a gospel concert on the Hampton Institute campus featuring Danniebelle Hall and The Rambos, I was elated. The fact that our group was going to be the opening act made the experience all the more exciting.

The day was Saturday, June 11, 1977. It was a beautiful, clear, sunny day, and the biggest opportunity to date for our group. Somehow I ended up sitting right next to Danniebelle. Playing on the PA system was "The Easter Song" by the group 2nd Chapter of Acts. In my nervous excitement of sitting next to this sister whose music I absolutely loved, I commented, "I love that song by 2nd Actor of Chaps." I was so embarrassed, and until this day I'm not sure whether Danniebelle noticed my flub. Dottie, Buck, and Reba Rambo took the stage, and Danniebelle lit up when she heard Dottie Rambo sing her classic song, "I Go to the Rock." After that performance, Danniebelle went directly over to Dottie Rambo and told her that she wanted to record that song. Danniebelle did record "I Go to the Rock" on her *Live In Sweden* album. Whitney Houston would also record that same song on *The Bodyguard* soundtrack album.

The next day, Danniebelle Hall gave a full concert at our church, and we had the privilege of being the opening act. After the concert, Danniebelle approached me and said she would like Living Sacrifice to be the backup band for her East Coast concerts. It was a dream come true. Sarah and I were married two months later on August 27, 1977. Sarah and Danniebelle became close friends through many long-distance calls between Hampton and San Jose, California, where Danniebelle was living at the time.

Our Wedding

Our wedding day.

In the church office, 1977.

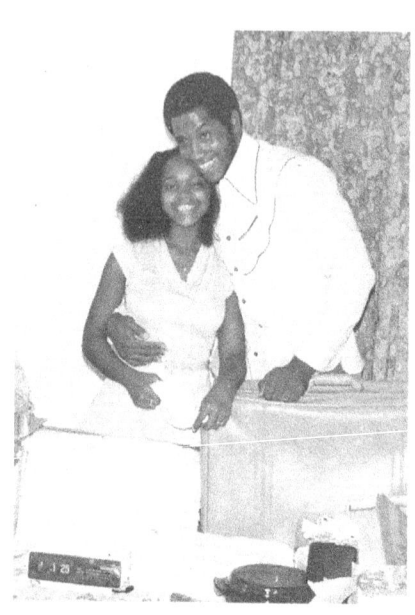

Wedding Day with gifts. 1977   Sarah with her mom on our wedding day.

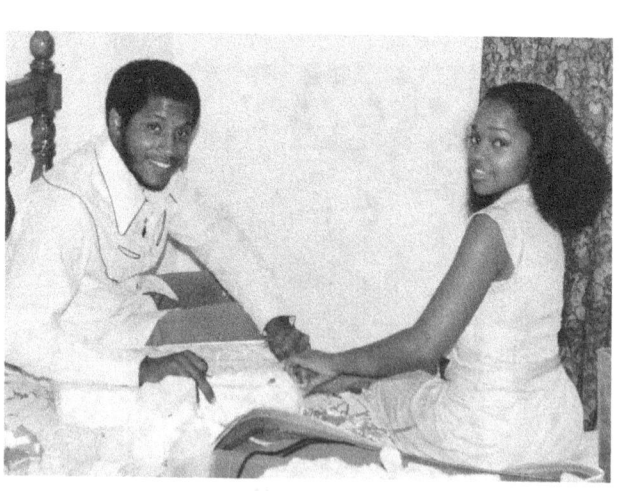

Wedding Day with gifts. 1977

Touring with Danniebelle

I was so excited when, just as promised, Danniebelle contacted me about the band joining her for three dates in the Northeast. The first was the Tremont Temple in Boston where she shared the billing with Edwin, Walter, and Lynette Hawkins. One of the most amazing occurrences that happened that night was when my brother Jonathan walked into Tremont Temple. As you can imagine, I was shocked and overjoyed to see him. His being there was an example of the hand of God and His ability to direct our steps. My mother had given

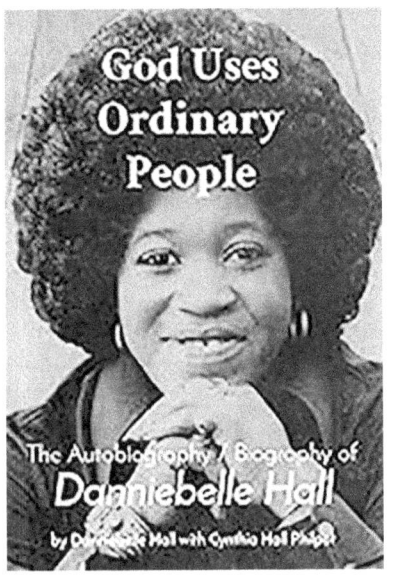

Danniebelle's Memoir.

him money to fly to Boston from Richmond, but he didn't even know where we were going to be singing. You talk about faith! He got off the plane, went to the downtown area, and just started walking around. He told me that to this day, he doesn't know how he found us!

We also performed at Queens College in Brooklyn, where I had the pleasure of meeting Lowell and Bea Carr. Bea was also one of the members of Andraé Crouch and the Disciples, and they had come out to see Danniebelle's concert. We also performed with Danniebelle at a New York coffeehouse that I thought was called the Lamb's Club, but in a published story many years ago about the account of events that I am sharing with you, someone contacted me and said I must have been mistaken about the location being the Lamb's Club. So, I will just say that we were the backing band for Danniebelle Hall in New York City at a coffeehouse sometime in the fall of 1978. We would later appear with Danniebelle in Hamilton, Ohio, at the Sonshine Festival and at Fishnet in Front Royal, Virginia.

Lesson in Generosity

In New York (at the unnamed coffeehouse!) we arrived early in the day to set up our instruments and equipment. We had parked in a parking deck across the street. A lady came into the coffeehouse begging for money to feed her children. I don't remember exactly how much I gave her, but I was moved by compassion to help her. As I was leaving the coffeehouse to go back over to the parking deck, I heard a voice behind me as I was going up the ramp.

"Hey," it said.

My first instinct was to just keep walking, and I did. He called out again, "Hey, you dropped your wallet."

I turned around to see this man standing there with my wallet. In hindsight I should have given him a reward because in that wallet was $1,100 cash. Danniebelle had sent me money in advance to cover travel, meals, and lodging for our mini tour. I can't help but think that this angel—or angel of a person—who handed me back my wallet was in some way associated with the mercy that I had shown to a poor stranger.

Demo Tape and Affirmation

Danniebelle had strongly suggested to me that our group should record a demo tape. Not long after that, we contacted Jim Michaels in Virginia Beach to do the recording. I sent the demo to Danniebelle, and sometime later she and Andraé Crouch were billed together at a concert at Rock Church in Virginia Beach. What a concert that was! Afterwards, I met Danniebelle down front at the church, and she started hastily walking towards the foyer, beckoning me to follow. When we got there, she looked at me and emphatically stated, "As sure as I am standing here, you are going to make it." This was an amazing affirmation. I considered her words to be prophetic at the time, and I still do.

Amazing Reconnection

In 1978, Sarah and I were still living in the Hampton/Newport News area when we heard that Andraé Crouch was going to be at the Richmond Coliseum. Andraé Crouch held a special place in Sarah's heart because at the age of fourteen, she gave her life to Christ while listening to Andraé's song "In Remembrance" on the stereo. This was our first time seeing Andraé Crouch in concert with a full band. The previous event at Rock Church had been primarily piano and vocal performances.

The concert in Richmond was absolutely marvelous. After the concert, we had the opportunity to go backstage and meet Andraé Crouch. My nephew, Mark Johnson, was with us, and as we approached Andraé, he looked at Sarah and said, "Hmm, pretty little girl." We laughed about that moment for years. I began to talk to Andraé and share some of the things about the call on my life for music and ministry. I noticed that Andraé looked over my shoulder and his face lit up as he pointed and said, "I tell you who you need to work with. This man." When I turned to see who he was speaking of, there stood Victor Torres! Yes, the same Victor Torres who fifteen years earlier had wrecked my eleventh-grade classroom with his powerful testimony. Indeed, we would later work with Victor Torres in an evangelistic crusade at Byrd Park in Richmond and also at an outdoor gathering at a farm for drug rehabilitation somewhere outside the city.

The Principles of God

Sarah and I attended a week-long seminar at the Hampton Coliseum in the summer of 1979. There were many principles we learned from the Word of God, but one in particular really made an impression on me: the principle of honor. I learned that honor is a principle God has set in place for the propagation of respect for authority; it's a safeguard against anarchy. I like to think of it this way: in the same way that grace is unmerited favor, honor is unmerited respect. We show it to whom it is due, particularly the authorities in our lives, whether they deserve it or not. The instructor went so far as to say that when we are relating to our parents, no matter what we think of them, we are to treat them like the parents we would like them to be. We should treat them as if they are already that person and as though they were God's authority in our lives. I learned just how powerful it is to take God at His Word. So, when the Word says in Ephesians 6:2-3, "Honor your father and mother, which is the first commandment with promise, so that it may be well with you, and that you may live a long life on the earth which the Lord your God gives you," He means it. Those who put their trust in His promises reap the fruits of obedience. I set out to apply this principle.

I had a two-week vacation from Howmet Turbine Components Corporation, and I offered to paint the house for my daddy; he was afraid of getting up on a ladder. To my surprise, he told me that he wasn't going to let me do it for free, and he was going to pay me the same amount that he would have to pay a professional painter. Right away I was earning more money than I would have earned working those two weeks at Howmet. Then the amazing spiritual fruit of the action began to grow. What I didn't understand then but would learn later was just how important it was to a man to be respected by those closest to him. It was obvious that this simple act of service had made a huge difference in my relationship with Daddy. On October 13, 1980, Sarah and I would move to Richmond with our new baby girl, Rachel, which began a whole new era of restoration for my relationship with my dad.

Medical College of Virginia

I landed a job again at the Medical College of Virginia (MCV), and in a matter of months I was promoted to supervisor of Patient Transportation, followed by a transfer and promotion to Supply and Distribution. God showed me His hand of protection as well as promotion during that time. The assistant director of the Transportation Department resented the fact that our boss favored me. She did everything she could to get rid of me, but everything she tried to do against me, my boss would defend me instead. When I was promoted to the assistant director in Supply and Distribution, my boss handed me the written reprimands she had put in my permanent record.

My job was obviously a way to support my growing family, but it would also be a platform for ministry. One of my greatest memories was standing in the linen chute collection room praying with William, one of the workers, to receive Christ. Sorting the linen that came down from all the floors in the hospital was probably the dirtiest job imaginable, and yet there we were. I began to go to chapel on my break to pray several times a day, and I began to see God moving in powerful ways in my growth as a believer.

It was also through that job I would have some monumental experiences. A Christian brother named Terry Guill who worked for an extermination company would come in and do regular treatments inside the Medical College complex. We became great friends, and when he came, we would go to the chapel and pray together on my lunch break. It was on this same job I prayed with my high school friend and coworker Reginald Cleveland to accept Christ. Reginald would later join the Air Force, serving twenty years as a chaplain. He later became a pastor.

The Demo Tape

Over the course of about four years, the demo tape we made at Danniebelle's suggestion had taken a real journey. It began with Paul Rogers, a sound engineer we had worked with at Harvest Place, a Christian dinner theater in Newport News. He sent it to Randy Bugg, who then sent it to Kurt Kaiser, who sent it to James Bullard. James Bullard had an assistant who absolutely loved the demo tape and told me, "I've got to hear this in wax," (meaning she wanted to hear the song on a vinyl LP album). She sent the demo to Gentry McCreary of Onyx Records, which was part of the Benson Company in Nashville, Tennessee. By now it was October of 1982. We had a brand-new baby, Jason, who was born on September 9 of that year. I had reached a place in my life where the realities of being a father of two and being twenty-six years old made me question whether I was on the right path as it related to music. Our band Living Sacrifice had for all practical purposes disbanded after Sarah and I moved to Richmond because of the seventy miles between the two cities. I literally came to a place where I had prayed and kind of apologized to the Lord for not hearing his voice correctly, and I decided I would go into the Air Force like my oldest brother Herman had done. I went to my parents' home to talk to my mother about what I had decided to do, and she listened to me patiently. Then she put her hand on her hip and said, "Boy, you'd better get out of here with that foolishness." Turns out, she believed in the call on my life even more than I did at the time!

The Telephone Call

The very next day after Mom rebuked me for wanting to give up and go into the Air Force, I went to work at my normal time as the three-to-eleven shift supervisor of the Patient Transportation Department.

Not long after my arrival, one of the secretaries said, "Gaines, there's a call for you." I answered the telephone, and on the other end was Nancy Nepola, Gentry McCreary's assistant, calling to tell me that Gentry McCreary wanted to sign Sarah and me to a recording contract. It was a moment of the most pleasant shock that I had ever had. So we headed to Nashville on October 14, 1982. Sarah and I, our two-year-old daughter Rachel, our one-month-old son Jason, and Sarah's sister Sherilla were on our way to sign our very first recording contract with Onyx Records and to begin recording our first album at the Great Circle Sound Recording Studio inside the Benson Company building.

I was surprised to discover that one of the first things we were scheduled for was a photo shoot for our album jacket. Gentry had paired us with a producer from Ohio. Let's just say that collaboration just did not work out. Gentry then decided he would pair us with another producer, Greg Nelson. Greg had produced Richard Smallwood's record on Onyx/Benson Records, and he thought that we would be a better match than the previous producer. We met Greg at Great Circle Sound Recording Studio,

This photo was taken October 15, 1982, at our first photo shoot for the cover of what was to be our first album with Onyx Records. That album, and this picture, were never released.

and he asked Sarah and me to sing for him. I played the grand piano in the studio, and I don't even remember what song we sang, but he loved it, and we were glad to be working with him as a producer.

The Wait

Because of the change in producers, we didn't start recording during that trip. We headed back to Richmond, and the painful wait began for us to return to Nashville and start recording our record, but there would be a lot of things that transpired. Amazingly, I told Danniebelle about our contract with Onyx/Benson Records, and she contacted Gentry and ended up being signed by Onyx records as well. I was elated that we were now label-mates. Time just seemed to creep by, but eventually I would be so grateful for that delay because of the things that were about to occur.

Abdominal Aortic Aneurism

That was the diagnosis. The patient was my father. My mother had a doctor's appointment with her doctor, Dr. Kumar, and while there she said to my daddy, "Herman, tell the doctor what you told me." Daddy just kind of laughed and made a joke out of it as usual, and said, "I told Bug (my mother's nickname) that my heart had jumped out of my chest and was beating in my belly." Dr. Kumar immediately looked disturbed and asked to check it. He took his stethoscope and placed it on Daddy's abdomen, listened, and told him he needed to schedule an emergency ultrasound. The ultrasound revealed that Daddy had an abdominal aortic aneurism that was so severe, it was ballooning with every heartbeat and actually protruding through his small intestines. Surgery was scheduled.

Crowning Moment

The night before Daddy's surgery, I went to visit him to pray for him. His good friend Mr. Clayton was in the room also, and I prayed and left. My mother would later tell me that after I prayed for Daddy and had left the room, he turned to his friend Mr. Clayton and said, "You see there, Clayton? My son is a real Christian." I can't begin to tell you how I treasured that statement. After all the years he was concerned about the direction my life was headed, he now was proud of me in front of his friend! It truly was a crowning moment for me.

Complications

The morning of Daddy's surgery, I went in to work just as always, and quite frankly I wasn't at all concerned about Daddy being in any real danger. I went over to my boss Phil Webb's office and just happened to mention that Daddy was having surgery to repair an abdominal aortic aneurism. He looked at me with shock and said, "Gaines, you shouldn't be here. You need to get to the hospital. That is a very serious surgery." I left work and headed to the hospital, and when I arrived I was informed that Daddy was out of surgery but had died on the operating table and had been revived. He was not conscious and was in great distress. I went into Daddy's room, and there he was, lying there with a grayish tint to his skin. Amazingly, I still was not worried. Daddy would lie there for more than a week in what seemed like a comatose state. The doctor then informed us that he had developed a high fever due to an infection. They told us if they did not break the fever, he would die. Their only option was to use steroids, but his intestines were not functioning, and the use of steroids would so compromise his immune system that he could die from almost anything. This was one of those situations where I believe God gave me the gift of healing. I felt the Lord was instructing me to go and lay my body over Daddy's body and pray for his healing. I waited until there was no one in his room, and I did just that. Before that day was over, Daddy's fever was completely gone. They did not administer steroids, and he regained consciousness shortly after that. To me, that was a clear sign of the hand of God healing my father.

Explain This

When Daddy regained consciousness, he told us he had died and that he saw his body on the operating table. He said he heard the voice of the Lord say, "You have not been right. I'm giving you another chance." There are other things that happened during that time that he would not tell us. My mother told me one thing he did tell her. To her astonishment, he told her the names of everyone who had visited him while he was unconscious and also the conversations that had been conducted in his room. She said to him, "Herman, there is no way you could know that." But he insisted. Daddy's life was radically changed after his recovery, and one of the greatest evidences was the love of God being manifested in his life. Before this situation, Daddy resented my cousin Dee. He felt that Dee had an inappropriate influence in my life and that I wasn't acting like a normal teenager because of my dedication as a Christian. Despite his feelings, he did not restrict me from going to church with Dee just a few blocks away from our home church where he was deacon and Mom sang in the choir. So when I went to my Aunt Ruth's (my mother's sister) home one day and saw Daddy sitting there having a conversation with Dee, I knew for sure the Lord had done a wonderful work in his heart.

Music City Dreams

April 1983, GMA

Ultimately, things did not work out with Onyx Records, and we were once again in search of a new record deal. When things went south, our producer, Greg Nelson, invited Sarah and me to come back to Nashville the following April for GMA Week (Gospel Music Association).

Greg Nelson is a legendary record producer, responsible for producing songs such as "More Than Wonderful" and "I've Just Seen Jesus" by Sandi Patty and Larnelle Harris, "People Need the Lord" by Steve Green, and "I Love the Lord, He Heard My Cry" by Richard Smallwood. Greg was also the owner of 19th Street Productions, which is the production company we were actually signed to as artists, and then contracted with Benson Company for distribution and marketing.

Our pastor in Virginia, Steve Stells, heard about the doors God had opened for us and our planned trip to Nashville. As a result, we were very pleasantly surprised with one of the greatest blessings we had ever received. During a Sunday morning service, Pastor Stells announced before the whole congregation that we were planning a trip to Nashville, and then he took up a love offering for us. I will never forget the feeling of love, support, and affirmation that this kind deed brought me. We now had more than we needed for our trip to Nashville, and this provision was one more indication that we were moving in the right direction.

I wasn't completely sure of the things that Greg Nelson had planned for our visit, but we ended up at 40 Music Square East at what was then Lorenz Creative Services. We met with Greg, Steve Lorenz, Elwyn Raymer, Michael Puryear, Charlie Monk, Scott Wesley Brown, and Phil Naish. I didn't know what to expect. I was nervous and excited. Then Greg just asked us if we had an accompaniment track with us. Of course I said yes and gave it to him. He popped it into the cassette player, hit play, and said, "OK, sing for us."

So there we were, standing in this room with some giants in the music industry, singing for them and not understanding the significance of that moment. Greg met with us after that impromptu audition and told us, "You guys have the talent, but you need the proximity to really develop as a songwriter. You guys need to move here."

That was not what I was expecting or wanting to hear, and quite frankly I was disappointed. We went back to Richmond and went on with life, but we prayed consistently for a seven-month period about whether moving to Nashville was the will of God for us. At the end of that time, our decision was made. We were Nashville-bound.

Prophetic Intervention

That same year, Sarah and I were invited to sing at Bethel Temple Assembly of God in Hampton. That night there was a minister there by the name of Dallas Plemmons. After we finished singing, he asked us to stand up because he had a word from the Lord for us. He prophesied that before that year had passed, we would see a major breakthrough in our ministry. He was right.

The Test

Sarah was three months pregnant with our son Nathan. The very next day after making the decision to move to Nashville and giving a one-month notification to my job, Sarah began to hemorrhage. We went immediately to the doctor, and they did an ultrasound. The news was not good at all. They pointed out to us on the ultrasound that Sarah's placenta had attached in a position that was covering the opening of her cervix. Their blunt advice was to abort the child. We never gave that a single thought, but we concluded that this was an attack and a test of our faith in God. We also believed it was a test of whether He was actually leading us to move to Nashville. Upon realizing that we were not going to accept the abortion option, the doctors prescribed total bedrest for Sarah for the duration of her pregnancy. As time went by and the date we were scheduled to move drew near, nothing had changed in Sarah's condition, but neither had our resolve and determination to move to Nashville as scheduled. We fully believed that this was not a matter of us asking God's permission to do something that we wanted to do, but rather the fulfillment of something that He had actually purposed for us.

The Move

Looking back, one of the things that I really found amazing was that my parents were so in agreement with us moving. My daddy was always super cautious about taking chances with the unknown, but in this situation I can say that we were all in agreement that this was of God. The most memorable moment about move day for me was that while Daddy was praying for us at the breakfast table at Mom and Dad's house, Jason, who obviously didn't have his eyes closed, in the sweetest and most concerned voice said, "Granddaddy's crying." I also cried then as Jason uttered those words, and I'm crying now as I write about that moment.

So, there we were, on our way with our two children, Rachel and Jason, and Sarah pregnant with Nathan. Our plan was to continue Sarah's bedrest plan once we arrived, but an amazing thing happened. The day that we moved to Nashville—November 16, 1984—the hemorrhaging suddenly stopped, and it stopped completely. At Sarah's first visit to the prenatal doctor for a checkup at Nashville General Hospital, the new doctors did an ultrasound and showed us that the placenta attachment was perfectly normal and posed no threat to mother or baby. We knew that was God's hand of protection over Nathan's and Sarah's lives.

Koinonia's

One of my first calls in Nashville was to Nancy Nepola, Gentry McCreary's now former assistant, to let her know we had just arrived in town. She invited us to come to Koinonia on Music Square East, a bookstore and coffeehouse next to Belmont Church. On that Saturday, November 18, 1984, WNAZ radio station was doing a live broadcast from the bookstore, and as soon as we arrived, Nancy met us at the door and asked if we had a track with us. When we said yes, she told us we were going to perform live on the radio. It felt truly unreal!

Shortly after we finished singing on the radio, I noticed a lady come in the front door with tears streaming down her face. She had been driving along listening to the radio while we were on air. She asked, "Who were those two people I just heard on the radio?" When we had been identified and introduced, she told us, "You are the voices I've been looking for to sing a demo of one of my songs." Her name was Suzannah Ryan Wilson, and the song was "Love Is the Reason," cowritten by Thornton Douglas Cline.

One week later, we were in the studio for our very first Nashville recording session. The demo would end up in the hands of Engelbert Humperdinck, and he would make the very first commercially-released recording of the song as a duet with Gloria Gaynor (famous for the song "I Will Survive"). We would also release this song on our *He'll Find A Way* album.

Nowhere to Go

When we first moved to Nashville, we were blessed with a completely furnished apartment. Jerry Thomas was a sales rep for Benson Records, focusing on the Onyx Records roster. He had a one-bedroom apartment in

Nashville that he used while in town working, and I happened to call him just as he was going to let the apartment go. The bonus was that he allowed us to have the television and furniture left in the apartment. Our blessing wouldn't last for very long though; we were notified by the rental office that it was against their policy to have a family with two children and one on the way living in a one-bedroom apartment.

So, there we were, basically being evicted. I was so concerned about this situation that I called my daddy and told him to hold the house next door open because we just might be coming back to Virginia. Fortunately, we were living off the savings I had from my job at MCV, and that would last us for a while as we sought musical opportunities. The problem was that from the vantage point of the rental manager, I was simply unemployed. I was frantically trying to find a place for us to live when I came across a telephone number advertised as an apartment finder. I called the number, and it was an automated system prompting me to enter corresponding numbers for choices, such as the number of bedrooms, and other options. I found a match, and when I went in to apply for the apartment, I explained to the rental manager that I was new to town and didn't have a job yet, but that I would not let her down if she took a chance on renting us an apartment. She listened patiently, and then said, "You know I can tell when someone is telling me the truth. I'm going to approve you for this apartment."

Warned in A Dream

I was busy trying to make connections in town and had set up an appointment to meet with someone. The morning of that scheduled meeting, Sarah told me she had a dream that the person I was scheduled to meet with had come to our door at the apartment, that she had answered the door with the security chain in place, and that this person had attempted to push in the door. For a number of reasons, I knew that this dream was a warning and that I was not to meet with this person. It was a test of my obedience because that meeting was the only sure thing I had. Should I go with the warning from the Lord or compromise for the sake of expediency? I chose to obey the warning.

I was able to make another connection, and now I was scheduled to meet with Debbie Fox of Paragon Publishing to talk about possibly becoming a songwriter for them. Her office was in the Benson Music Building on the second floor. After my meeting with Debbie, I took the elevator down to the first floor to exit the building, and as soon as the elevator door opened, there was Greg Nelson, the producer who had suggested we move to Nashville, with a shocked look on his face. He said, "I can't believe you actually moved here!" and told me to look him up now that we were in town.

The Hustle

No, not the dance, but the work ethic! My first job after arriving to Nashville was working as a supervisor in Rivergate, and this was a far cry from my last job at MCV as the assistant director in Supply and Distribution/Linen Division. It was work, though, and readily available.

My next job was with Pinkerton Security as a security guard, and it was the first time ever that I would shave the beard I had worn from the time I was able to grow hair on my face. On March 20, 1985, while guarding a new apartment construction site on Murfreesboro Road, I was sitting in my van in pitch darkness, blocking the entryway to the construction site, when my supervisor contacted me to tell me that Sarah had gone into labor. I left immediately, and at 6:20 the next morning, Nathan was born.

I had put in numerous job applications in my job search, and amazingly that same day I received a call from Parkview Hospital to come in for an interview. When I arrived, I was interviewed by a lady named Edwina Temple. She turned out to be the daughter of the legendary track coach who had coached Wilma Rudolph to Olympic gold. My previous experience in hospital work gave me an advantage, and I was hired as a supervisor in the housekeeping department. It turns out that my new salary was comparable to my salary at MCV, and I had not lost any ground in that regard. In addition to my job at Parkview, I would also hustle and do other jobs, like changing Michael Puryear's universal joint and Elwyn Raymer's brake pads in the parking lot of Lorenz Creative Services. I had also met Chris McCollum who was a sound engineer at Great Circle Sound, and I would take a painting job that he had contracted for Calico Corners Store in the Green Hills shopping center. Those seemed like random jobs at the time, but the hand of God has a way of bringing things back around in the future.

While at Parkview I was inspecting one of the doctor's offices and happened to see a picture of the doctor and his family and noticed Amy Grant was one of his daughters. Shortly thereafter we were attending a Sandi Patty concert at the Tennessee Performing Arts Center. When I turned around, right behind us was Amy Grant. She was one of the kindest human beings I had ever met. From that point on, wherever I would see her, she always remembered me and greeted me warmly. Years later I would do harmony lines with Amy on the chorus of her song "Somewhere Down the Road," and Sarah and I would also record our *Come on Back* album at her studio, Tehas, on her farm.

The New Deal

Eventually we signed an artist development deal with 19th Street Productions and Lorenz Publishing. There I was, songwriter by day and hospital supervisor by night. One thing I learned was the benefit of being around professionals, those who had already succeeded at what I was trying to accomplish. The synergy of being around gifted people only made me better at what I was doing. I then really understood what Greg meant about proximity. Some of my fondest memories were of the Monday writers' meetings where we would come in and play the songs we had worked on that week. One of the most memorable songwriters' meetings was when Steven Curtis Chapman and Phil Naish, his producer, played Steven's first single on Sparrow Records, "Weak Days."

Greg had paired Sarah and me with a new producer by the name of John G. Elliott. We began our musical collaboration, and when I played him a song I had begun writing back in Richmond, he lit up with excitement. I had the chord structure and melody but no lyrics, but after all the amazing things that the Lord had done for us in bringing us to where we were, I knew that this song was supposed to be about

His faithfulness. It was as if the song was writing itself. John was so excited, he asked to write the bridge to the song. We were on our way to being a great team. When we finally had a chance to present "You Are Faithful" at one of the writers' meetings, it was a great thing to know that a song born right there in Washington Park, on Akron Street in Richmond, Virginia, would soon be recorded and would be heard worldwide through radio and television.

We were off to a great start, and we were soon in the studio to begin tracking (recording instruments) for our first three songs that also would serve as our demo to acquire a distribution deal. Simultaneously, Sarah and I also began working as recording session singers. In addition, I started recording vocals for commercial jingles with Hummingbird Productions. Soon we would get great news. Mike DeMonico and Dan Cleary signed us to a distribution deal with Milk and Honey Records. I was now poised to start receiving a weekly draw (advance salary) so that Sarah and I could dedicate our time solely to finishing our first album.

Celebration

It was August of 1985. We had landed our first distribution deal and were ready to start recording for our upcoming debut album with Milk and Honey Records. We were heading back to Richmond to share all the good news and celebrate. Going back to Virginia was always a celebration. We could expect that when we arrived at my mom and dad's house, my mom would have fried chicken and macaroni and cheese and green beans waiting on the stove for us. Nathan was now six months old, and this trip would be my parents' first time seeing him. Nathan was so alert and advanced that when my dad saw him, he said, "That ain't no baby, that's a little man." You have to understand that Nathan started walking at seven months old! We were able to share with our family all the wonderful things that the Lord had done for us. We had our three-song demo, and we also had other recordings that we had done. One was a Doublemint Chewing Gum commercial in which I had sung a duet with Kim Fleming, and a Chevrolet commercial that I sang was airing in the Detroit market. I also had a demo that John Elliott had hired me to do of his song "That's Where the Joy Comes From" that Steve Green had recorded. We were quite happy and looking forward to getting back to Nashville. I had resigned from my job at Parkview to devote myself full-time to music and finishing our new album.

The Telephone Call

In the midst of our wonderful celebration with family, I received a telephone call at Mom and Dad's home. It was Elwyn Raymer, the head of Lorenz Creative Services, asking me if I could get my job at Parkview back. He went on to explain that Zondervan had bought Milk and Honey Records and dissolved the company. I wasn't certain what would happen with Mike DeMonico and Dan Cleary, who had done the distribution deal for our upcoming album. One thing was certain, the completion of our album and the weekly draw (salary) was out of the picture. This was devastating news; the celebration was completely deflated, and we faced some real uncertainty. What happened next, though, would forever change my life.

Remembering

As always, I would approach everything in my life with prayer and consulting God. This situation was no different. I told Sarah what had happened, and we prayed. I was really down-hearted and sad about these new developments, and it was now time for us to drive back to Nashville. But the Lord spoke to me in my spirit and told me to begin to thank Him for all the things He had done for me, starting at the beginning of my life as far back as I could remember. I began driving, and I am sure that the Holy Spirit was bringing things back to my memory that I didn't even know I could remember. We were driving on I-64 West, and the distance between Mom and Dad's house to the I-64 West and I-81 South junction is roughly 135 miles. By the time I took the ramp to I-81 South off of I-64 West, I was so full of faith and absolute joy that it was unimaginable. Remembrance and gratitude had lifted me up out of the mire of doubt and despair. The drive between Richmond and Nashville is ten hours, and by the time we arrived back in Nashville, I had concluded that this was yet another test we had to face head-on by faith. For decades now, prayers of gratitude have been a part of my life, which is the reason I can write these accounts in this book.

Back In Town

The Sunday after we arrived back in Nashville, we went to our home church, Belmont Church. Dan Cleary saw me in the foyer. He approached me with tears in his eyes and told me, "I'm so sorry about what happened, but if I'm ever in a position to do something about it, I will." He then put a $100 bill in my shirt pocket. I would never forget the empathy and concern Dan showed me that day.

I felt from the Lord that if we would put the kingdom of God and ministry first, that He would add everything else to us. One of the things that our three-song demo had afforded us was the ability to share our music by cassette tape. I had already sent copies out to a number of churches and had scheduled appearances for after what was going to be our initial album release date. There was still money in our recording budget to do final mixes of the three songs. I had an idea, and I presented it to my writing partner, John. I told him that instead of spending that money on finishing the first three songs, I wanted to spend it on tracking for the seven remaining songs so that we would have simple tracks to use for the ministry engagements that we had already scheduled. He said that was highly unusual and he didn't think Elwyn Raymer would approve it. Once again, we prayed and asked God for favor, and to my delight, it was approved. We were now in full-time ministry and traveling extensively. Not only that, but the Lord blessed us and caused us to prosper. At the end of that year, we had received three times my annual salary at Parkview.

Dan Cleary Surprise

Zondervan was already the owner of The Benson Company and Benson Records. The acquisition of Milk and Honey Records resulted in Dan Cleary now working for Benson Records as the head of Artist and Repertoire (A&R). True to his word, Dan Cleary was in a position to "do something about it," and signed us to Benson Records. In our first meeting for planning the completion of our record, we had a conversation about our three-song demo. He said something that shocked me. He said, "It wasn't the three-song demo that sold me on you guys, it was the "Love is the Reason" demo that Greg Nelson played for me before you even recorded the three songs." In that moment I realized that with all of our effort to record in hopes of creating something that would garner us a recording contract, the fact was the very day we arrived in Nashville—when Suzannah

Ryan Wilson heard us on WNAZ and hired us to sing that song—was the moment we were entering a destiny where God had already gone before us to prepare the way.

A blast from the past 1986 Nashville TN background session for our first Album (and I do mean vinyl album) with Producer John G. Elliott First Call members Melodie Ware Tunney and Bonnie Keen sang bgv's on "He's Risen In Me" "You are Faithful" "Come Drink At My Table" "Glory To God In The Highest"

Circa 1986-Signing Day for Billy and Sarah Gaines with the
Benson Company. Biily and Sarah Gaines,' Elwyn Raymer of
Lorenz Creative Services,; John Taylor, VP of Marketing at
Benson; and Dan Cleary, VP of A&R.

John Birdwell, Sarah, Billy, Tom Granger (editor
and Associate Publisher for CCM magazine)

Marty McGeheee (4 Him), Producer/songwriter Don
Koch, Thomas (Dee) Todd, Karen Todd, Me, Sarah,
Angelo Petrucci (Angelo and Veronica), and Brian
White at the Benson Company

Living the Dream

Hometown Homecoming

It was the summer of 1986, and we had finished our very first album earlier that year. It was simply titled: *Billy and Sarah Gaines*. We were booked to sing at the Arthur Ashe Athletic Center in Richmond as the opening act for Phil Driscoll. This was our first event where we would have our brand-new album for sale. My heart was filled with gratitude. Here we were in my hometown where I was born. There could not have been a more hoped-for scenario than this for the introduction of our new album.

As I was driving through Colonial Heights, Virginia, on I-95 North with my radio tuned to WDYL radio station, I suddenly heard the intro of our song, "He's Risen in Me." It was our very first radio single. I must admit, I was smiling from ear to ear. All I could think was here I am in my hometown, riding on I-95, and for the first time ever I hear our song on the radio! It was the fulfillment of the prophetic dream I had back in 1975 when I heard my voice singing through the stereo! The concert that night was one of the most memorable times in my life. The joy of having my mom and dad and other family members there for that event made it all the sweeter.

The Power of a Song

Just in case you missed it, both Sarah and I came to the Lord listening to a song. For her it was Andraé Crouch singing "In Remembrance," and for me it was Kate Smith's "Room at the Cross for You." I've shared the amazing interventions of the hand of God that brought us to this point in 1986. Ultimately, the whole purpose of the Lord bringing us to the platform of the music industry is really very simple. It was to deliver the gospel through song.

Another key person God brought into our lives at that time was Andy Ivey. I met Andy at a recording studio on Music Square West, and I remember him telling me that he was going to be our new radio promoter at the Benson Company. Andy would later be our A&R director, as Dan Cleary became our producer. Andy's task was to help us choose our third radio single. By this time, we had already released "He's Risen in Me" and "You are Faithful" as our first two radio singles. John Elliott had brought me the song "Come Drink at My Table" when we were initially choosing songs to record. The song was written by Justin Peters and Sandy Dixon. Initially I rejected the song. It was in the style of a country music arrangement, and I guess in my mind I couldn't hear past the arrangement. John said, "I just ask that you take the tape home, learn the song, and then sing it in your own style."

It has often been said that country music and R&B music are cousins, and it is true; it was as if this was a song I was born to sing. Andy suggested that we release "Come Drink at My Table," so we did. I will always remember going to Lorenz Creative Services to pick up my mail and finding a letter from a young man who stated he had been contemplating suicide when he heard "Come Drink at My Table" on the radio, and it changed his mind. Radio chart position status, awards, and record sales all pale in comparison to the reward of knowing that through the power of a song, God allowed us to touch so many people. Through the years we have received thousands of letters, emails, and social media messages as testimonials of the power of a song.

Jason's Surprise

As time progressed, I decided to modernize my songwriting with new technology, namely MIDI (musical instrument digital interface). I had purchased a new MIDI keyboard, a sequencer, and a drum machine. It was now 1987, and Jason was five years old. While working on my new equipment and still trying to figure it out, Jason would stand behind me, watching my every move. One day he asked, "Daddy can I touch that drum machine?" I turned to him and in the politest and most fatherly way possible explained that these instruments were what Daddy used for his work and that they were not toys.

He insisted, "Daddy, I just want to touch it one time."

I said, "Okay. Go ahead."

This boy played a drum pattern that was so complicated and intricate that I almost fell off my seat. In that instant, I realized this little genius was already more advanced than me in his abilities to sequence music, and I just got out of the way and let him flourish. He would co-write a song with me, "That's the Life," and probably became one of the youngest members of ASCAP (American Society of Composers, Authors, and Publishers) ever.

Just Kids Playing

Jason taking over the studio—and I do mean taking over—would turn into an unexpected blessing. He became a magnet for other young musicians, and our home became a little haven for other kids to come and work. From my vantage point, they were just kids playing. When we first moved from Hampton back to Richmond in 1980, the first church that we attended was Faith Landmark Ministries. There we met Delise Kimmey and her three girls, Lisa, Andrea, and Joy. Sarah would end up being their babysitter. I couldn't have imagined what this connection would turn into. Sometime after we moved to Nashville, Delise and her three girls moved to Nashville also. So when Lisa and Jason were in the studio, they again were just "playing," that is, until Lisa, Andrea, and Joy became the group

Out Of Eden on Goatee Records. Kara Williamson, Mandy Omartian, and my daughter Rachel became the best of friends and also became the group Prelude. They were signed to Michael Omartian's label, and he was the producer of their debut record. Another young man in and out of our studio was Darryl Fitzgerald, who was later a part of the Christian rap group Transformation Crusade on Benson Records. Darryl and his wife Stephanie have three children, twin girls Alexis and Alexandria, and their son Darius. Sarah and I had the honor of being chosen to be their kids' godparents. In 2016, when I saw that those kids, along with Nicole C. Mullens' daughter Jasmine, had been signed to Capitol Christian Music Group as the group The New Respects, I began to see a pattern. We were blessed to have these young

Father's Day: Mandy and Michael Omartian, Rachel and me, Kara and Dave Williamson

Rachel and Jason (bottom left and right) with Lisa, Andrea, and Joy Kimmey.

musicians in our home who eventually went on to have success, and to see our son Jason writing and programming music with them.

Nathan and The Knife

Another story about God's supernatural intervention through dreams happened in 1987. Sarah was taking a nap and had a dream that Nathan had a knife in his hand and was standing at the top of the staircase. Then he fell and cut himself. She woke in a panic and ran to the living room. There she found Nathan standing at the top of the steps with a butcher's knife in his hand. She got to him just in time to avert a potential disaster.

My Family and Wheels

My mother hated motorcycles, so when I pulled up to her home towing a Yamaha Bayou 4x4 ATV on a trailer behind our van, she took one look and said, "What did you get that thing for?" I completely understood her sentiment. I'd heard the legendary stories of her brothers and their injuries on motorcycles. My Uncle V.T. (Virginius T.) Johnson was driving a three-wheel motorcycle when it flipped backwards, injuring the back of his head. My Uncle Phillip Johnson had broken his leg so severely riding a motorcycle that my mother said his leg was turned around backwards. My brother Jonathan slipped in some loose gravel while riding a motorcycle, resulting in his leg being pinned with the motorcycle on top of it and the exhaust pipe burning his leg. Although my mother didn't know, I was an eyewitness to my brother Herman riding a motorcycle with my nephew Nathaniel on the back and popping a wheelie. Nathaniel fell off the back, but fortunately had the coordination and athleticism to hit the ground running. He never fell to the ground; he just ran, caught up with the motorcycle, and jumped back on to the back.

So, back to my ATV. I decided to take it for a spin on the old ball diamond on Jasper Road, close to the entry of Forest Lawn Cemetery in Washington Park. There was also an old dump at the edge of the ball field. I was doing laps around the old ball diamond, with Jason on the back of the ATV. I was applying the brakes and slowing down while driving on the edge of the field bordering the old dump, when suddenly the two front wheels dropped into a rut that was covered by brush. With the front brakes already applied, it caused the ATV to tip forward as if it was in slow motion. Jason was thrown over my back and landed six feet out from the ATV. I was thrown off and landed on my left side with my right shoulder up and perpendicular to the ground. Just as I thought to myself that I was sure glad we didn't get hurt, the ATV, which had been standing on end with the front grill against the ground, slowly tipped over and came crashing down on me.

It probably wouldn't have been so bad, except the ATV weighed 695 pounds, and when it hit me, I felt my left collar bone forced up over my shoulder joint. I was in shock, and still so grateful that Jason was not injured. As I crawled from under the ATV, it was obvious to me I had a serious shoulder injury. Amazingly, and probably due to the combination of shock and adrenaline, I was able to turn that ATV back over on its four wheels and pull the handlebars that had been flattened level with the seat back up in the original position. We hopped on and I drove back to the van. As I pulled up onto the trailer, the front wheels of the ATV hit the front rail of the trailer. I recoiled backwards, holding on to the handlebars for dear life. As I was thrown back, my left collar bone was pulled back into place.

My sister Jane drove me to the hospital, where they were able to bandage me up. The doctor told me I would have to exercise that shoulder for the rest of my life, or I would develop arthritis in it. That became one of my greatest sources of motivation to continue working out. I was truly grateful Jason and I were both wearing helmets, and that he in particular was not harmed at all. I must say, though, that I felt so badly about putting my child in potential danger that I had flashbacks of the event, complete with alternate worse endings. There were a number of times I was awakened in the middle of the night with dread over what could have happened. It could have been much worse, and for that I am truly grateful that the hand of God protected us.

Christmas 1987

Every year at Christmas we would drive back to visit family in Virginia. Christmas for me was, and still is, the most wonderful time of the year. It was extra special now, though, because it was also a family reunion of sorts. One thing different about this Christmas was that my mom was in bed the whole time we were there. She had slipped on ice while walking outside and had severely strained her groin trying to keep from falling. It really made me sad that she wasn't up and around and enjoying all the festivities, but she was happy as ever that we were in town and that we and the kids were enjoying our Christmas there. I didn't really think any more about the situation until about a month later when I received a call from my sister Barbara. She told me my mother had been diagnosed with lung cancer and it had spread to her brain. I collapsed and fell to my knees in shock and fear. I couldn't help but wonder if my mother's being bedridden at Christmas was actually associated with this illness, and that in her typical selfless way, she didn't want to ruin Christmas for us with bad news. Later that night, I called my dad to talk to him, and the sound of his voice and the agony of his wailing on the other end of the line was terrifying and sent chills through me. I could barely even make out what he was saying. That night, Dan Cleary came over to present some new songs for the *He'll Find a Way* album we were currently working on. I couldn't even think straight, and the last thing on my mind at this time was choosing songs.

The Fight

After the initial shock of it all, I was ready to believe God for a miraculous healing for my mother. We planned a trip back to Richmond, and I called Pastor Steve Stells and asked that he and the elders of the church come and pray for my mother's healing. He so graciously agreed, and when I arrived at the hospital, he and the elders were already there. The next day, my father and all my siblings met with my mother's oncologist, and his words were devastating: "We don't want to try anything heroic." In other words, this cancer is terminal, and there is nothing within reason that we can do. But I could not accept that determination from the doctors to be the final word. My mother had always shown such strength, determination, and belief in crying out for others when they were in trouble. Now she needed someone to cry out for her. I had seen her plow through many situations in prayer to receive answers, and I was hopeful and determined for the same outcome.

We went back to Nashville, and I found myself crying and praying every day in the shower, I guess in hopes that maybe a shower would wash at least some of the sadness from my face. I called my mother every day after that, and she was always full of faith and confidence. On March 3, 1988, I received a call from my sister Mary Kathryn informing me my mother had died. Earlier that morning was the last time I ever spoke to her. Her words to me were, "I will not be defeated," so you can imagine that news of her death was shocking. My brother Jonathan would later tell me that one week before her death, she told the family that "whether I live or whether I die, I am His." He also said that even with her weakened lungs, she had sung the song "Take Your Burdens to the Lord and Leave Them

There" with a voice as clear as a bell. The night my mother died, they were all gathered at my mom and dad's home where my mother had a hospital bed in the den. After she died, Daddy climbed in bed with her and held her body and wept bitterly. My brother Jonathan went out in the backyard and said that he could hear the voice of the enemy ask the question, "Well, what do you think of faith now?"

I hate death, but I must tell you that the greatest manifestations of God's presence and power in my life have been in His comfort in lifting me from grief when it seemed like I just couldn't humanly overcome it. There was a story that my mother told me of a fourteen-year-old boy who lived in our neighborhood whose mother had died and that the boy grieved himself to death. This was evidence of the potentially negative effects of grief. But God, by the evidence of His resurrected son Jesus, gives us hope that we don't have to be overcome with hopeless grief; on the contrary, He comforts us by His promise of our resurrection. When we die, we are taken away alive. In death, we are living in eternal existence with Him.

Underlined

Sometime after my mother's death, Sarah and I and our children were sitting at the breakfast table having prayer and Bible study, which was our daily norm. I happened to look over at my daughter Rachel and noticed that she had what looked like my mother's Bible. Sure enough, it was her Bible. I had never really had any reason to look through it, but at that moment, it was comforting to hold something that had belonged to her. I was further comforted as I began to thumb through the pages and saw where she underlined and highlighted passages of scripture. I wrote the song "Underlined" to describe my feelings.

Underlined

VERSE 1

I found my mother's Bible, it was just the other day
I watched the treasures of her heart unfold with every page
She had underlined the words of truth she wished to emphasize
I found myself all teary-eyed yet pleasantly surprised
Well she's gone to be with Jesus now, of her thoughts I can't inquire
But I could not have found more clear a written will of her desire

CHORUS

Underlined were the words about commitment
Underlined were the words about contentment
Underlined were precious promises that calmed her doubts and fears
Underlined were words that spawned the love she'd shown throughout
the years
I remember most the things she emphasized
I knew her heart by things she underlined

VERSE 2

I still can plainly hear her say, "Son, you follow God"
Like passing an eternal torch to light the path I trod
Traces of her teachings find their way in all my thoughts
A proof that God has granted her the answer that she sought
Looking back on all she did, one thing comes to mind
The reoccurring theme of love that her life underlined

CHORUS

Underlined were the words about commitment
Underlined were the words about contentment
Underlined were precious promises that calmed her doubts and fears
Underlined were words that spawned the love she'd shown throughout
the years
I remember most the things she emphasized
I knew her heart by things she underlined

BRIDGE

She could not have known

There's no way she could see

That those simple underlines

Would mean so much to me

CHORUS

Underlined were the words about commitment

Underlined were the words about contentment

Underlined were precious promises that calmed her doubts and fears

Underlined were words that spawned the love she'd shown throughout

the years

I remember most the things she emphasized

I knew her heart by things she underlined

Rachel's Ranula

Rachel developed a ranula under her tongue. A ranula is basically a stopped up salivary gland. It was like thinly stretched ballooning of the salivary gland under her tongue. I can't begin to tell you just how distressing this was for me, especially when the doctor told us the only way to correct it was by surgery. One of the saddest days of my life was seeing my little twelve-year-old girl lying on a stretcher outside of the operating room. The surgery went well, however, and we were thankful and grateful for the miracles of medical science. But not very long after that, Rachel developed another ranula, this time on the other side of her mouth, under her tongue. This was another one of those situations I would have to say God gave me the gift of faith for healing of this particular illness. I felt that this was a spiritual attack, and I prayed for a miracle, that God would heal her. The ranula disappeared; no surgery needed the second time!

Danniebelle Full Circle

In 1991 we released our third album *No One Loves Me Like You*. Included on that album was the song "The One Within." One day while at home I received a surprise call from Danniebelle Hall. She told me that she was driving along listening to the radio, and that she heard a song by me that caused her to pull over to the side of the road because she was crying so hard. I told her, "Danniebelle, I got that song from you." I explained to her that in 1977 I was watching the *Ross Bagley Show* on the CBN network and saw him interviewing Danniebelle. She began to talk about inner healing of the child inside, and in that moment, the concept for the song "The One Within" was born. Danniebelle was shocked and delighted to hear that her words had inspired that song.

After I had watched the interview that day, I heard Sarah sitting at the piano and playing a beautiful melody and chord progression. I asked her where she got that from, and she said she made it up. I was surprised and told her how beautiful it was. I asked her to show me on the piano how she was voicing the chords (the position of her fingers on the keys) and asked her if I could use it as the chorus of a song. She agreed, and I wrote the music to the verses and the lyrics to what would become "The One Within." We began singing it during our live performances, but we didn't record the song until 1991.

It's amazing to think that Danniebelle sowed a seed by her words in that television interview, those words germinated in my heart, then took root and grew into a song that would bear fruit of encouragement to her fourteen years later.

The One Within

Within lives the person we really are
And there he lies broken, battered, and scarred
Rarely making known the hurts that harbor there
Pretending not to care, but is it true
Jesus came and for our sins He died
And to free the captive that is trapped inside
Every sorrow now in faith to Him reveal
Asking him to heal the one within

CHORUS

Lord hear the one that holds his peace and seldom has his say
Lord mend the bleeding heart grown cold from the hurts of yesterday
Rebuild the one torn down by all of the blows of life and sin
Lord heal the broken one that lives within

VERSE 2

Oh don't hide the pain that you really feel
Cast your cares on Jesus and He will heal
All the scars and bruises that you have unveiled
For He has never failed and He never will

CHORUS

Lord hear the one that holds his peace and seldom has his say
Lord mend the bleeding heart grown cold from the hurts of yesterday
Rebuild the one torn down by all of the blows of life and sin
Lord heal the broken one that lives within

More Open Doors

New Deal

I was praying earnestly that God would open new doors for us and for a way to work with producer Michael Omartian, who was out of the range of our recording budget at the Benson Company. While I was in prayer one day, I got a call from an attorney named David Epstein who told me he had found what I had been looking for. It turned out that he connected me to funding for our next project. *Come on Back* was produced by Michael Omartian and yielded one of my most enduring songs, "Other Side of this Trial." I wrote the song in 1993 while going through one of the most intense trials of my life. In the middle of that trial, I could sense the Lord speaking to me, telling me that on the other side of this situation I would be a better man and that I would have a stronger relationship with him than ever. And that's just what happened.

Other Side Of This Trial

VERSE 1

I stand at a river, I must reach the other side
Don't know how I'll get there, the river's cold and deep and wide
So strong is the current, I 'd be surely swept away
Stronger though is my Father's hand and He will make a way
This trial is that river, but I've been here before
I've learned from the last time, That I will reach the other shore

CHORUS

On the other side of this trial I'll be a better man
I will know the sweet deliverance of my Father's mighty hand
I will have another battle won upon which I can stand
I'll grow closer to my Savior as I trust His Master Plan
I'll know Him better, I will be better, I'll be a better man

VERSE 2

I cried with my whole heart, My God what have I done
To deserve what I'm going through, He said it's just that you're my son
I'm doing a work in you, building patience in my child
You will find on the other side, that it's all been worth the while
So hold on to My promises as you watch My will unfold
You'll see that this trial was under My control

CHORUS

On the other side of this trial I'll be a better man
I will know the sweet deliverance of my Father's mighty hand
I will have another battle won upon which I can stand
I'll grow closer to my Savior as I trust His Master Plan
I'll know Him better, I will be better, I'll be a better man

BRIDGE

Now I'm not talking about the sweet by and by
But in this here and now He'll deliver me somehow

Jesus Take the Wheel

The first time I heard this song by Carrie Underwood, I thought to myself, "Somebody must have read my story and used it in this song." Years earlier, I had written the following account in an email that I had sent out to a number of people.

Sarah and I and our three children were enroute to Kansas City, Missouri. I was driving our Chevrolet Suburban on I-70 West in the left lane when a pick-up truck towing a trailer suddenly swerved out of the right lane and into the left lane right in front of me. I remember thinking, "Why would anybody do something so stupid!" As I applied my brakes, I could feel the vibration in my brake pedal of the anti-lock brake system activating due to a loss of braking traction. What seemed like a perfectly clear road was actually covered with an invisible sheet of ice. It's called black ice. There was no way possible for me, at my present speed and with the remaining distance between our vehicle and the trailer in front of me, to avoid plowing into the back of the trailer. My only option was to drive to the left into the median. There was probably about six inches of snow on the ground in the grassy median, and it quickly became obvious that this bumpy, slippery, snow-on-grass median was even more dangerous than the black iced pavement that I had just left. I did everything I could to steer the vehicle, but it was as if the steering wheel was worthless. I literally took my hands off of the steering wheel and I cried out, "Lord, help us!" We careened out of control, rotating laterally, going all the way across the median and heading for the opposing traffic in the eastbound lane of I-70. We nearly missed going into oncoming traffic, then spun back toward the center of the median, with our vehicle now traveling backwards and gradually slowing to a stop. I cried out, "Thank you, Lord!"

As I looked to my left, I saw that all the traffic on the westbound side of I-70 had been completely shut down by state police due to a solid, glistening patch of ice that stretched across the road. There were flood lights illuminating the whole area of the road. Just beyond this shutdown was the empty westbound interstate. I put the vehicle in gear, engaged the four-wheel drive, and made a left u-turn in the median. I was able to drive past the ice patch on the interstate by driving parallel to the road while still in the median and drove back onto the pavement. In my rearview mirror was the sight of blue police lights, flood lights, and the headlights of a multitude of stopped vehicles that had turned that stretch of interstate into a virtual parking lot. We drove on to Kansas City that night completely unharmed, with no damage to the vehicle.

Promise Keepers

It was May 1997 that I attended and sang for three Promise Keepers Conference events in three different cities: Tampa, Chicago, and Seattle. This event had a major impact on my life because of the principles and teachings of integrity that were shared. It was also the largest gathering of people I had ever sung for.

One of the most memorable lessons from that conference was an illustration that one of the speakers made. He set up several bear traps on the platform stage, opened the traps in their spring-loaded, ready position, and then demonstrated the power of the trap by setting it off with a stick. He then blindfolded his son and had him place his hands on his back. He navigated his son around the stage, weaving around the set bear traps. The message was powerful. We as fathers, because of our vision, are able to help lead our sons around traps that we can see, but that they cannot see. This principle is broadly applicable, not just in the father and son relationship, but in anyone who is a mentor helping to guide others away from dangers they can't perceive.

One of the other blessings that came out of this movement was the principle of racial reconciliation. In a conversation with one of my Caucasian friends, he told me he believed I was the person of another race he was to have a covenant friendship with. That friendship still remains, and that brother has been one of the greatest blessings in my life to this day.

Rice Broocks Change of Plans

One of the most unusual things that ever happened to me was on a flight to Baltimore/Washington Airport. I saw Pastors Rice Broocks and Tim Johnson from Bethel World Outreach Church in Nashville in the airport terminal, and when we recognized each other, we talked for a few minutes. Pastor Rice is the author of *God's Not Dead*, which was later made into a movie. He asked me where I was headed, and I said Norfolk, Virginia. For the first time ever, I had someone ask me to change my travel plans. He asked me to travel with him to New York City. A short while after the terrorist attack on the World Trade Center, Bethel World Outreach had planted a new church in New York City. So there I was, changing my plans completely, getting in a rental car, and driving from Baltimore/Washington Airport up to New York City. The drive was about four hours, and we talked the whole time. I knew that this was a divine intervention, and it wouldn't be long before I had a clear understanding of what this intervention was about. Pastor Rice spoke so much encouragement to me on that trip, at a time when I really needed to be encouraged. I was frustrated that our ministry opportunities had stagnated, and I will always remember when Pastor Rice told me he saw me as a big ocean liner that was temporarily in harbor to be cleaned, and that God was going to take that ship and send it out to the world. Then he apologized and qualified his next statement by saying, "I'm not calling you a dog, but I see you as a dog that isn't mean, but in an attempt to make the dog mean, people beat the dog." As much as some people might have been insulted by such a statement, I wasn't, because I knew that this was the Lord speaking to me through a parable and an analogy that was very fitting for what I was going through at that time.

Alone

It is not good for man to be alone, and if there were ever a man to whom these words fit, it was my father. It was torturously heartbreaking to see my father living alone after my mother's death. Though he was amongst family, some of whom actually lived only a few doors away, the loss of the companion who had so fit him was obviously visible in his countenance. My mother and father were true companions, and in their latter days shared everything. They seemed to be glued together; they reveled in the empty nest, and I remember how much they enjoyed going out to dinner to places like Duff's Buffet. One of the sweetest stories I ever heard was from my cousin Wanda, who told me she had driven out to Washington Park where I grew up, and she spotted my mother and father walking down the sidewalk holding hands.

We were fortunate enough to be able to fly my father to Nashville to visit with us periodically, and I know that was always a refreshing time for him. When my dad would visit, it was almost as if we had exchanged roles. If I left the house without taking him with me, I would find out later from Sarah that he was upset that he was left behind. He was fortunate enough to have a pension from his old job set up as an annuity that was paying him monthly, and it met all of his needs. So when I heard that he had gone back to his old job to work, I was a bit puzzled. In his now widowed life, I wanted to do everything I possibly could to bring him comfort. I didn't want him to toil all the rest of his days, so I asked him how much he was making on that job, and he told me the amount. I said, "Daddy, I don't want to see you have to work all of your life, so I will give you whatever they're paying you monthly so that you don't have to keep working." I didn't know it then, but what I considered to be a gesture of love and kindness was actually one of the worst things that could ever happen to him because now he found himself profoundly alone. One of the saddest conversations with my father was when he told me that there were some days the only voice he heard was his own. Oh, how heartbreaking that was for me to hear! Going to that job was actually good for him because of the social interaction that he had with others, and the other employees enjoyed and looked forward to seeing my father, with his comical teasing and prodding of his coworkers.

The loneliness began a downward spiral for him emotionally, which turned into a physical complication, also. It contributed to him developing dementia, and it was so difficult watching him fade away right before our eyes. He died at home with my sister Jane caring for him. I am thankful to know that he had the wonderful comfort of one of his children there with him till the very end.

New Chapter in Life

---◆---

The Move Back to Virginia

It was the year 2000, the beginning of a new century and of a new chapter of our lives. Our daughter Rachel was twenty at this point, and our sons were eighteen and fifteen. Ministry opportunities had dwindled in Nashville, and we needed to make some changes. We had made connections in Norfolk, Virginia, and were offered a role in starting a new record company. We were excited to be able to help with a whole new generation of artists in their development. It didn't work out that way, though. We had moved everything we owned in two tractor trailer moving vans to Virginia Beach with the understanding that our moving expenses would be paid for. We were staying in a motel in Newport News, with two trucks full of our belongings waiting to be delivered. The only problem was we did not have the $13,000 that we owed to have everything delivered and unloaded. It was the greatest pressure I had ever faced, and while Sarah and the kids were visiting her relatives in Newport News, I knew this was one of those get-alone-with-God, intense-prayer-time situations that I had to face alone. I went back to the hotel room, fell down on my knees, and cried to God for His help. While I was praying, the Lord impressed upon me a person to call. I can remember vividly that

I received the return phone call while I was pumping gas at a nearby gas station. Some of the sweetest words that I ever heard were the words of my friend: "Billy, man, I'm so sorry to hear what has happened to you. I'm overnighting you $4,000 to help with your living expenses. And I will contact the movers and pay them directly for the $13,000 that you owe."

Ziklag

I can remember crying in the shower every day and having a sense of shame, feeling like I had made one of the biggest mistakes of my life in moving back to Virginia. To add to my grief and despair, Rachel decided to move back to Nashville by herself, stating that she was "going back to where God called her." Those words shook me to my core. While I was in prayer seeking the Lord regarding all of these things, I heard one word in my mind: Ziklag. I had no idea what that word meant, but my search would lead me to 1 Samuel 30. David and his men had been at war, and when they returned to their city, Ziklag, they found that the Amalekites had attacked it, burned it with fire, and taken all the women and children captive. While all the men wailed and talked about stoning him, David cried out to God, strengthening himself in the Lord. When he inquired of the Lord, asking if he should pursue the Amalekites, the Lord answered, "Pursue, for you shall surely overtake them and without fail recover all" (verse 7). David and his men chased after their enemies and attacked them, rescued their wives and children, and brought back all of their stolen belongings. "And nothing of theirs was lacking, either small or great, sons or daughters, spoil or anything which they had taken from them; David recovered all" (verse 19).

The message was clear as a bell: go back to Nashville and recover all. We had been in Virginia only four months. Three friends in Nashville heard about our plight and gave us the funds—another $13,000—to move back to Franklin, a city just south of Nashville.

Mama's Answered Prayers

It was Saturday, September 27, 2003. I was at the airport headed up the jetway to board my flight when I received a call from my cousin Wanda informing me that she had gone to visit my brother Loon (Herman). She said he was ill, and the way he looked scared her. This gave me great concern. When I landed back in Nashville on the following Monday, as I was walking down the jetway, I received another telephone call, this time from my brother Jonathan, letting me know that my brother Herman had died earlier that day. I was stunned. But what he said next was truly amazing. He told me that on that Sunday, the day before Herman died, he had a strong sense he should visit my brother, not knowing that he was gravely ill. He and his wife Carolyn decided to go that Sunday night. When they arrived, he realized just how ill Herman was. Herman asked my brother Jonathan to pray for him. In the course of that prayer, Jonathan asked Herman if he was sure of his salvation, and he prayed with him. The next day, my brother was gone. I knew instantly that this was an intervention of the hand of God. My mother had said often, "Your brother Herman is going to come to the Lord. I might not be alive to see it, but I know that he will." She was so sure of her prayers and that God had heard her regarding the salvation of her children.

What's even more amazing to me is that Jonathan was the one the Lord used to usher Herman into the kingdom of God. Around 1974, my mother, my brother Jonathan, and I were in the kitchen. She began prodding my brother about surrendering his life to the Lord totally, and his reply was, "Momma, if I want to go to hell, that's my business." Both my mother and I stood there in stunned silence. I don't even remember a word after that statement. But my brother did surrender his life to the Lord totally, and in November of 1987, with my mother and father present, Sarah and I sang at his ordination service and heard him deliver his ordination sermon. That was a moment of sheer elation for me, and I commented afterwards, just before our closing song, that this was one of those moments in life where if I died at that moment, I would die with great joy and a sense of great fulfillment in my heart. This same boy who made that statement to my mother was now standing there as a man of God, declaring the gospel of Jesus Christ. And that same boy, years later, brought our brother Herman to Jesus.

It was four months after Jonathan's ordination that Mother would be in eternity, but her prayers still live on and are manifested in my life, even as I write this. I'm sharing this story with my brother Jonathan's permission because he has quietly had a prison ministry for the last thirty years where he preaches to prison inmates. He is a great reminder to me of the fact that the good our Heavenly Father sees us do in secret will be rewarded to us openly. I want to encourage those who are praying for the salvation of loved ones that just as Abraham did not consider his old age or the deadness of Sarah's womb when he considered God's promise, we should not consider the hurtful things that the loved ones we are praying for say or do. Instead, we must remember that God who has promised is able and faithful.

The Austin Wranglers

In 2004 I received an offer from Greg Feste to be the Director of Entertainment for the Austin Wranglers Arena Football Team and also to head up a new music company. This time the offer was real, with a great salary and benefits. I was primarily responsible for the entertainment during half time shows for the home games that were held at the Frank Erwin Center on the campus of the University of Texas in Austin. This was one of the most fun jobs I had ever had. Not only did I get to choose talent for the half time shows, but I also got to perform and sing in them as well. But in the overall scheme of things, I was there for a purpose other than what I had imagined. I moved to Austin, and Sarah moved there later after closing down her in-home day care center she had started. While there, I met and worked with Jed Seneca, Greg's right-hand man. It would only be six months before a restructuring of the company led to widespread layoffs. I was one of the casualties of that layoff. The silver lining was that I received a severance package, and all of my moving expenses and temporary housing costs were covered by the company. But it was the connection to Jed Seneca that would prove to be one of the most pivotal connections for me in the years to come.

Ten Thousand Angels

In 2001, after returning to Nashville from our brief time in Virginia, Sarah decided that she wanted to pursue a career in childcare and did not want to be involved in travel and ministry any longer. She went back to school, got a degree in early childhood education, and started a daycare center in our home. From that point, except on very rare occasions, all of my ministry appearances were strictly solo.

I decided to do a hymns project with just vocal and piano. Bernie Herms was highly recommended by a friend, and I contacted him to see if he would be interested in working with me on this project. He agreed, and I was delighted. I had a list of all the songs that I wanted to record, and as we went through each of the songs, I sang them as we worked out arrangements, tempo, keys, and the overall feel that I wanted for each song. As he played, his musical instincts were absolutely amazing, and I knew that we were on to something. Bernie took extensive notes and told me that he was going to go and refine the arrangements further. We had a recording studio in our basement, and when Bernie came over to record the piano tracks, it was absolutely mesmerizing. He did not use any sequencing at all. He played every song live, with no overdub or punch-ins, from top to bottom flawlessly.

Jed Seneca had moved from Austin to Indianapolis and had taken the position of worship leader at the Every Nation Church pastored by former NBA player, Dave Jameson. He invited me to come up to Indianapolis to minister in song for a Sunday morning service. Jed was also a recording engineer, and we had talked about him recording the vocals for my hymns project. He had a Pro Tools studio in the back of the church, and after the

Sunday morning service and lunch, we went back to the church to record my vocals. I have never had a recording session that I felt was as God-inspired. I stood there and sang all ten songs live, back-to-back, and I could not believe the acoustics of that simple room. It was as if it was designed just for me. I brought the vocal and piano tracks back to Nashville, and Michael Omartian's engineer, Terry Christian, did the final mix on the project. Tess Erwin, who had been our publicist at the Benson Company, did the album design, and in 2006 I released my first solo album, *Ten Thousand Angels*. The album was distributed through Central South Distribution through a connection with Terry Wood, and then through Millennium Entertainment. Bill Traylor was the owner of Millennium Entertainment, but he was also the President of Benson Records when we recorded our first album with Benson. *Ten Thousand Angels* was the first album of which I owned the masters, and amazingly, I earned more in sales royalties than all our other album sales combined. To this day, I still receive quarterly royalty payments from the *Ten Thousand Angels* album.

Monica's Miracle

The trip to Indianapolis was one of the rare occasions when Sarah would travel with me, and it would be one trip that she would forever be grateful for. When we went out to lunch after the church service, a lady sat across from Sarah by the name of Shelley Harris (now Shelley Rusk). In her conversation with Sarah, she mentioned that there was a medical center out west in Arizona that dealt with the terminally ill. Monica Winston, who was our live-in nanny for many years and like a second mother to our children, was very ill at the time and needed an intervention to preserve her life. Sarah did the research on this center and read the testimonials of many patients who had been helped by the treatments. The treatment was quite expensive, though. Sarah told a friend about Monica's situation and began to cry, telling her she didn't want Monica to die. The friend told Sarah, "Don't cry. I'll pay for it." Sarah was elated and was Monica's travel companion, staying with her through the whole process of her treatment. The treatment was a great success.

Christy Meeks

I was doing very well with the release of my first solo album, and I was receiving calls from friends letting me know they were hearing a number of songs from my album on Moody Broadcast Radio, the Oasis Network, and on SiriusXM Satellite Radio. On Saturday, November 11, 2006, Christy Meeks contacted me by email through my website's concert information portal, inquiring about my requirements for making an appearance at a church. As the worship leader of her father's church, Evangel Assembly of God in Gainesville, Georgia, her father had commissioned her to find someone to sing for an anniversary service. What I would learn later was that her father had requested a Southern gospel group because the church could not afford to pay a lot of money for someone else. When I replied to her email inquiry with my requirements for coming (travel, lodging, meals, and a love offering) she was quite pleasantly surprised.

I was scheduled to minister in song on Sunday, December 3, for the morning and evening services. This was another one of those rare occasions I was able to convince Sarah to travel with me for an engagement. The morning mini concert went well, but something that I dreaded and hadn't mentioned to Christy happened. She begged Sarah to sing. I would learn later from Christy that Sarah's reply to her begging was, "You sing with him." After the service I received an envelope with a love offering, and I was shocked at the generosity of the church. I wouldn't know until nine years later that Christy's husband Steve had gone back to the room where the love offering was being counted. He said, "OK, now, this is Billy Gaines, and we can't give him just any kind of love offering." Obviously, his advice was heeded because it was unlikely that a love offering from that congregation would have equaled that much.

When Christy and Steve were in college at Southeastern University in Lakeland, Florida, they would regularly hear our music played on WCIE radio station. They said that they had become big fans of ours and they also sang our songs. They were a wonderful couple, and Sarah and Christy really connected with their love of children. At this point, Sarah was doing child daycare from our home, and Christy was working for Babies Can't Wait, a Georgia state early intervention program for babies with learning disabilities. The pleasant experience of ministering at Evangel Assembly of God placed it high on my list of churches that I would regularly check back with to see if there was a possibility of returning. I would learn later that Christy was very frustrated with me at dinner that night because she wanted to hear stories and information about the music industry, and all I talked about was just normal stuff. I laugh about that even as I write this. But she would eventually hear a great portion of what I have written in this book. I couldn't have dreamed what the future would hold for all four of us.

Virginia Again?

Yep, this time for a completely different reason. It was September of 2008. Times were tough for us, and we were living in a rented townhouse. On September 29, 2008, the stock market crashed, and quite frankly I wasn't really concerned at all as to how it would affect us personally. Sarah was still doing a daycare from our home, and I was still traveling and ministering, and as long as there was an airport nearby, I could easily fly out to my engagements. I never would have imagined the impact the crash would have on the decline of ministry opportunities.

When Sarah's mother received a court settlement, Sarah wanted to go to Virginia to use the money to renovate her mother's home. Rachel was married by this point, and Nathan had moved to Los Angeles to pursue his career. Sarah and I, with Jason, temporarily moved to Virginia for what was supposed to be a three-month home improvement project. It ended up stretching out to more than a year, and I was desperate to find work. As a Tennessee resident, it was very difficult finding work in Virginia in a now-suppressed job market. When things became critical for us, I was desperate to get back home. I had booked a Christmas concert for December in Crestview, Florida. I had my plane tickets already and was expecting that we would be back in Nashville by December, so I had to change my flight to fly out of Norfolk International Airport. The day of the trip gave me a lot of time driving in my rental car, and I prayed earnestly for help from the Lord. I arrived in Crestview, Florida, and the concert was wonderful. When I finished my concert, I got a call from Sarah's sister Sherilla. She told me that Sarah had broken her ankle earlier in the day, but she didn't tell me because she knew that I would have turned around and come back home. She knew that we needed the money.

I flew back home the next day and found that Sarah was in a lot of pain. She had a cast and would be pretty much immobilized for six weeks. Months seemed to drag by as I was overseeing the construction project and driving to pick up supplies for the renovation. In May of 2009 I was contacted by a concert sponsor in London, England, who invited me over to do a mini tour in several different cities. I had to drive all the way to Washington, D.C., to get my passport in time. He offered to pay for Sarah to travel with me, but she declined. It was a wonderful tour with an awesome live band, and I also made some great new friends. Basil and Rajae Reid treated me like royalty, and the hospitality they showed me made me feel at home. It was a great time of ministry and my first tour as a solo artist with a band. I came back to Virginia actually feeling refreshed and rejuvenated.

On August 2, I prayed earnestly that God would intervene on our behalf and open the doors for much needed resources. Not long after that, I got a call from a friend and recording artist I had known for years. He asked me how I was doing. When I told him I was doing OK, he asked me how I was really doing. I said that I felt like the bottom had dropped out of my life. He told me that he was overnighting me a check for $2,000. It couldn't have come at a better time and showed me once again God's hand of provision.

Back to Nashville

Back to Nashville

I decided to travel back to Nashville to search for a new place to live. I never dreamed that when I kissed Sarah goodbye on August 4, 2009, it would be our last kiss ever. When I returned to where we were staying, she was gone. As I said in the introduction, this book isn't intended to be a full account of all the events of my life. I will therefore not discuss the particulars of our separation because Sarah can no longer answer for herself. All these years later, I have simply decided to focus with gratitude on the thirty-two years we had together as husband and wife. With all of the ups and downs, good, bad, riches, poverty, sickness, health, peace, and controversy, I'm still grateful for the time we had together. I am convinced that God purposed our lives to be together for matrimony and ministry, and that death should have been our only separation. But the one thing that is necessary for this kind of covenant to be sustained is to mutually agree in its significance, its sacredness, and its purpose as the will of God.

I will say that it was a devastating separation for me. My daughter Rachel was now married and pregnant with her daughter, Olivia; Nathan was living in Los Angeles, and Jason was still in Hampton. Sarah and I both moved back to Nashville, but separately. When I was invited to sing for the funeral of one of our friends' children, Sarah was there as well. I turned to walk away from that graveside feeling the lowest that I could have ever imagined, and the bagpipes that were playing seemed to exacerbate my sadness even further. As I was walking back to my car, someone called my name. When I turned to look, it was David "Smitty" Smith. At my very lowest moment, the Lord had this angel of a man waiting there for me. We began to talk, and he told me that he'd been looking for me. Smitty was truly a friend sent from God to help me. He eventually connected me with Pastor Patrice Gordon, the pastor of City of David Church. In my brokenness and loss, Pastor Gordon still believed in the irrevocable call of God on my life and offered me to be the worship leader for the church. He would later say, "Every Sunday morning for months you cried, and we cried with you," and that was no exaggeration. This church family truly bore my burdens with me in their mercy and love.

As time progressed, it became clear to me that Sarah and I would not be reconciled, and after four years and four months of separation, our divorce was final on December 19, 2012. Pastor Gordon told me that he wanted to meet with me after my divorce was final, and I was shocked by what he asked of me. He said that because Sarah and I were married for a long time, I owed it to her to give her a year in the event that she changed her mind. That meant no dating or pursuit of any relationship. And though I was surprised, I believe that yes, we do need to obey those who have the rule over us, and those who are legitimate godly authorities in our lives when we know that they are watching for our souls and have to give an account for us. It's one of the ways we see the hand of God working in our lives.

Reroute

In the fall of 2011, I had decided to buy a chest freezer and a pop-up tent to do some concession sales. I had good success with this while in Hampton for the renovation of Sarah's mother's home, and I wanted to try it again in Nashville. While I was in line at Sam's Club purchasing the freezer and pop-up tent, I noticed a lady in front of me had one of the large, flat carts loaded down with so many bulk food items that I figured she must own a restaurant. I asked her about it, and she turned out to be the owner and operator of Ella Jean's Cafe. The conversation led to the revelation that I was a singer, and it ended with an invitation for me to come and sing at the restaurant once a week. Later that day I somehow received an advertisement for a PA system that was 50 percent off. It was an amazing deal and something I needed for my new weekly engagement at Ella Jean's Café. So, the next day I returned the freezer and the pop-up tent and purchased the PA system instead. I would go on to use that same PA system for the Sunday morning services and as a worship leader at City of David Church. I have to say that it paid for itself many times over. I share this to illustrate that even when we feel we are making the best decision we can at the moment, we must always keep our hearts open for God to redirect us. This is a GPS navigation term, but I believe it kind of sums it up. If it were not for the Lord hitting the redirect button on the GPS of our lives, we would never reach our destination. The hand of God redirects our path.

Pastor Rob Mallan

It was Sunday morning, May 12, 2013. I was at Christian Family Church in Tampa, Florida, and I had just finished singing the song "No One Ever Cared for me Like Jesus" from my *Ten Thousand Angels* CD. After I left the platform, Pastor Rob Mallan began speaking.

"I know that Billy doesn't know this," he began, "and neither do most of you who are here this morning, but when I was seventeen years old, I got in some trouble and went to jail. While I was in jail, the chaplain gave me a Billy and Sarah Gaines CD. This man was my first gospel music influence in my journey to Christ."

I was floored. The congregation was shocked also. In that moment I realized once again the amazing grace and redemptive power of the gospel of Jesus Christ set to music. It was just one more situation that would seem like fiction if I hadn't lived it.

Moving On

A year passed. It was now December of 2013. There was no change in the status of my relationship with Sarah, and I remember thinking to myself that I was glad I listened to my pastor, if for nothing else than to know I was surrendered and still willing to be reconciled. I was in a state of mind that I was simply pursuing the kingdom of God and ministry and didn't have any relationships, dating or otherwise. Actually, I had come to a place where I had resolved in myself that I might be single for the rest of my life.

On January 14, 2014, I was scrolling on Facebook and saw a picture of Steve and Christy Meeks. I liked the picture and didn't think any more about it. The next time the picture appeared in the news feed, I read the caption and found out that posting was actually an announcement about Steve's sudden death. I felt like a fool for liking the picture instead of taking the time to make a comment offering my condolences. I removed the like and called Christy to offer my condolences and to ask what happened. My heart broke for her and her children as she gave me the details of Steve's death. Without much thought, I made the statement that can seem so cliché at a moment like this, "If there is anything that I can do, please let me know." To my surprise, she said there was something. She hadn't spoken to anyone about singing for Steve's funeral yet, and she asked me if I would be willing to do it. I said yes. We talked more and planned that I would also sing for the Sunday morning service at Life Point Church. She also asked me to bring the accompaniment track for "In His Eyes" and said that if she felt up to it, she would like to sing that song with me.

When I arrived on Saturday for a sound check before the funeral, I walked into the funeral home chapel and heard someone playing the piano.

I thought to myself that it sounded like Larry Goss's style of playing. It was Debbie Stevens Palmour, and we talked and decided that she would play for me when I sang instead of using my accompaniment tracks. While I was getting my sound check, Christy walked into the chapel from the back. My heart broke for her even more. It was as if she was bewildered. I greeted her, and it seemed at that very moment there was a conversion of two grieving hearts, mine for my loss of my marriage to Sarah and hers for her loss of her husband and father of her five children.

It wasn't long after that people began to file in for the service. After it was over, I got separated from the funeral procession to the graveyard, and I drove to Life Point Church where the repast was to be held. Once inside, Christy introduced me to the husband-and-wife physicians whose home Steve was working at when he collapsed. They told me how they had administered CPR instantly, to no avail. After the repast, we went into the sanctuary to get a sound check for the following morning service. I realized while we were practicing "In His Eyes" that this was a moment of distraction from Christy's grief, and I was happy I could help provide that for her.

The morning service went very well, and we did sing "In His Eyes" together. After church I went out to lunch with Pastor Dave Allman and his wife Liz, Christy, and some of their Southeastern University college friends. I made my way back to Nashville that evening. Sometime later I got a message from Christy that Evan, her oldest son, was cleaning out his father's truck and he found a copy of my *Ten Thousand Angels* CD. I am pretty sure that CD was the one I had given to Steve when I was there for my 2006 concert. Christy told me Steve loved that CD. Here again I was truly grateful to know that God had used me in Steve's life as an instrument of encouragement.

The Telephone

Nashville was 300 miles away from Gainesville, Georgia, so the telephone became the primary means of communication between Christy and me. I called her about one month after Steve's death, and I must say I was very surprised at just how open Christy was about how she was feeling and the challenges that she was facing now being sole parent and provider for her four children still at home. She

would later write that my first function in her life was as a counselor. That really was a true statement. She was so open and straightforward as she poured out her heart that I knew one thing for certain: she trusted me. She seemed to know intrinsically that I would never betray her confidence. From my vantage point, I knew God had sent me into her life at a crucial time for her, and that my purpose was to be an encourager and a cultivator. We began to pray together, and her faith was being strengthened by recognizing just how the hand of God was moving on her behalf.

June 12, 2014

It began as just a normal day, other than the fact that I felt tired and knew early on this would be one of those days that I would need a nap. I was scheduled to sing for a funeral service for the brother of Lisa Gordon, the wife of Pastor Patrice Gordon. My plan was to go to the repast after the funeral to eat and fellowship for a while, and then go and take a nap before going to pick up my grandchildren Olivia and Briley. I was then going to take them to Rivergate Mall to ride on the carousel and get chicken and fries, which was our ritual. For some reason I never heard any word about a repast and I assumed that there was none. I headed home to make my lunch, which cancelled out my much-needed nap. I had just purchased a new car the day before. The timing belt had slipped on my existing vehicle, and a few months earlier I had to replace a head gasket, so I knew that at 150,000 miles, this was an indicator of more repairs to come.

When I arrived to pick up Olivia and Briley to take them to the mall, Olivia asked me, "Gandy, why did you get a new car?" As I tried to explain, she said, "I'm not ever going to ride in this car again." I was absolutely baffled as to why she would say such a thing. We headed to the mall, and while there, I became so exhausted that I had to cut our time short. I headed back home and still didn't get to take a nap. I decided I would go to the building where we had our church services and pick up my PA system because I didn't want to fight rush hour traffic in the morning. On my way back, I was driving on I-65 North, fighting sleep, and anxious to get home. I took the Old Hickory Boulevard exit, and as I approached the traffic light to make a left turn, it was still green. The last thing I remember was thinking to myself, "Good, it's green, and I won't have to stop for that light." The next thing I remember was an impact that was so severe, it nearly knocked the wind out of me and caused my teeth to clack together. I saw the deployed and now-deflated air bag that my face had just hit, and I could smell the distinct odor of what I recognized as stage fog, the kind of fog that you see at a concert. The front of my car was crumpled, and there was a mist in the air, most likely rising from my ruptured radiator.

I had fallen asleep at the wheel and run head-on into a concrete wall on the right-hand side of the road just feet away from the ramp leading back on to I-65 North. My first thought was why, but before I could even finish that thought, praise and gratitude broke through. I remember saying to myself, "No, I'm not going to ask why, but thank you, Lord, that I am alive." Immediately I looked in my rearview mirror, and I saw the blue lights of a police car right behind me. I remember wondering how he got there that fast. As the policeman exited his vehicle and approached mine, I forced the jammed driver's side door open. He asked if I was OK, and I said yes. It was only when I got out of the vehicle that I noticed I had pain in my chest and my lap area from the seatbelt impact. The policeman told me that he was just one car behind me when I hit the wall.

It seemed that in no time there was an ambulance and paramedics there. The paramedic saw me walking around and said, "Hey, buddy, you shouldn't be walking around." They laid me very carefully on a board, put a collar on my neck, and taped my head to the board to hold it still. I arrived at the emergency room, and the battery of tests began. After X-rays and a CAT scan, the technicians informed me that I didn't have any broken bones. While still lying on the CAT scan machine, I asked if I could use the bathroom. I saw blood in my urine, and when I told the technicians about this, they said they needed to do another scan, this time of my abdomen with a contrast dye. The technicians informed me they could not identify from the scan any visible damage that would cause bleeding. The emergency room doctor wanted to catheterize me to look into my bladder. I asked him if there was any other option, and he said they could test my urine in the morning for blood. I said I'd take that option. I was admitted, and by the time I was settled down in my room, the pain was so severe that I needed pain medication.

The following morning, I was joyful because I didn't see any blood in my urine. I told the nurse, and she said they still needed to run a test and that my visual observation was not adequate to determine with certainty the absence of blood. They took another urine sample and sent it off to the lab to test it. There was no blood, and I was discharged from the hospital. As I was getting dressed, I looked in the mirror and saw a big purple bruise across my lap. After things had settled down and I had time to think, I realized that it was miraculous that the policeman was right behind me when I hit that wall and that he was able to stop the oncoming traffic immediately. Where I crashed was perpendicular to the road, and the back three-fourths of my vehicle was across the acceleration lane. The oncoming traffic's direction of approach was on the other side of a crest of a hill. Without the traffic being stopped by this police officer, someone could've come over that hill and not been able to stop in time before hitting my vehicle.

My car was towed to a collision center, and I waited to see whether it would be a total loss as I had suspected. Sure enough, it was, but I was shocked when I learned what the settlement would be. The car only had 167 miles on it when I crashed. I had paid $6,000 less than the sticker price for it, but the settlement was for the full sticker price. It was unbelievable that I had just received a check that was $6,000 more than what I had paid for that vehicle!

Move to Gainesville

By July of 2014, my friendship with Christy had grown into a romantic, loving relationship. Though there was no engagement ring yet, we both knew that we would be married. I moved to Gainesville, Georgia, but I was still commuting weekly

between Nashville and Gainesville in my role as the worship leader for City of David Church. I would eventually take a position as worship leader at Victory Temple Atlanta Church, with Pastors Mark and Merisa Davis. We

Christy and me with Christian music artist, Carmen.

began to attend Free Chapel in Gainesville for the Wednesday night services. Pastor Jentezen Franklin was reading the passage beginning with Ephesians 5:25: "Husbands, love your wives just as Christ also loved the church and gave himself for her that He might sanctify and cleanse her with the washing of water by the word." While he was still reading, Christy turned to me and said, "That's what you do for me, you wash me with God's Word." It was in that moment that I had the greatest sense ever of being valued for the essence of my being. Her words were a healing balm and an indicator of what she treasured most about me. There is so much that I could say about Christy's and my relationship that would be a whole book in itself. However, it was becoming clearer than ever that my purpose in Christy's life was not just romantic but a divine appointment.

The Deer

I was traveling from Gainesville to Nashville on Interstate 75 North at about 5:00 a.m. on Saturday, October 25, 2014. I was in the left lane when I noticed headlights in my rearview mirror getting closer and closer. I decided to move over to the right to allow the vehicle behind me to pass. Just as I merged into the middle lane, I saw a deer crossing the road from right to left. I didn't even have time to brake. I clipped the left hind quarter of the deer with an almost glancing impact. I pulled over to the side of the road to inspect my car, and I remember thinking, "It doesn't look that bad." I was able to complete my trip to Nashville without any further problems. When I thought back on that incident, though, I realized that if I had not moved over to allow that other vehicle to pass, that deer, at the rate that it was traveling, would have been just about dead center of my vehicle in the left-hand lane. At 70 miles an hour, a collision like that could have been deadly. One thing is for sure, the damage to my vehicle would have been substantial. My heart was filled with gratitude once again for God's protection.

Grief-Driven

Grief-driven is the terminology I used to describe why my relationship with Christy progressed so quickly after her husband's death. I appreciate people who talk to you instead of talking about you, who ask questions instead of assuming or drawing conclusions devoid of facts. My son-in-law Brian is one of those people, and when he and Rachel asked those questions, that's the response I gave. It had been five years and six months since Sarah and I had been separated, and one year and one month after our divorce was final that l had gone to Gainesville to sing for Steve Meeks' funeral service. The connection with Christy began with sharing of sorrows. I felt that I had known her all my life, and her present sorrows were consistent with a path that I

had already walked. Both of us had now lost a spouse we loved, and both of us had faced foreclosure and the loss of a home. Both of us had lost a substantial amount of weight, and we could both identify with a newfound sense of life and vitality that is also accompanied by its own set of pitfalls.

But it was the coexistence of deep grief from losing a spouse and falling in love with someone else so soon that would be the most controversial element of our relationship. Add to that the fact that I was a Black man and she was a White woman, and it was a sure formula for raised eyebrows and disapproval. There is something to be said about the concept of love languages, though. If a person's love language is touch and affirmation, none of the other languages will ever truly suit them if that one element is absent. You can't cook, clean up, work hard, or provide well enough to make up for the lack of affirming words, affection, and intimacy. Christy and I both had the same love language, and we spoke it fluently. Christy loved to talk to me, and she loved to hear me talk. Many times, I would say something that really moved her, and her body language and her countenance were as if she had just melted a little. Most of the time as a kid when your parents called you by your full name, you knew you were in trouble, but in Christy's case, when she would pause and say, "William Harvey Gaines," the air of expectancy was always resolved with her next statement, "I love you," and that always melted me. Once, when some of the criticism about our relationship seemed overwhelming, she said, "Well, we've been praying that if our relationship is not of God, that He would reveal it to us. Maybe the opposition is a sign that we should not get married." On a number of occasions, she said that she wanted God's will above all, and that if

there was any way that Sarah and I could still be reconciled, she would want that, especially for my and Sarah's children. I assured her, though, that not only was Sarah done with our marriage, she had no interest in marriage to anyone.

We would eventually submit ourselves to the counsel and authority of Christy's father, Pastor Gerald Jordan. I loved visiting Pastor Jordan because there was a tangible presence of God whenever I walked into his home. I loved him because he was straightforward and honest with me, and his reply to our question of what he thought about the opposition that we were facing was, "Now both of you have said repeatedly that you believe that your relationship is the will of God for your lives. I will admit that I wasn't too excited about Christy marrying a Black man, but I know that you are a godly man and that you both love each other. All I ask is that you love my daughter and treat her right." After Christy and I were married, I would have to say that spending time talking and praying with her dad were some of the very best times of my life. Shortly after we were married, I had awakened one morning very early, and while still lying in bed, I began worshiping and praying under my breath. Or so I thought, because out of the silence and darkness came Christy's sweet voice, "You don't know how good it makes me feel to hear that." I would come to realize one of the reasons she loved me was that my dedication to the Lord reminded her of her father, whom she loved dearly.

Georgia on My Mind

————————◆————————

Marriage and Ministry

On February 21, 2015—my birthday—Christy and I were married, and eight days later on Sunday March 1, 2015, we went on our very first ministry trip as a married couple to Zephyr Hills, Florida. Shortly after that, on March 25, 2015, we were invited to be a part of the filming of Nancy Harmon's *The Jesus Connection*. I could not help but think just how elated my mom and dad would have been to have seen me singing on her program. My dad had passed away in 1997, a decade after my Mom. While they were alive, they watched Nancy Harmon every Saturday night on television. I found favor with Nancy, and she asked me to do a number of solos during the filming. This was one of those moments I knew God had orchestrated. Here I was in Atlanta at WATC TV 57, singing on the *Nancy Harmon Show*, working with someone I had watched thirty-some years ago in my hometown. It was quite surreal. Being married to Christy and being involved in these new ministry opportunities together gave me a great sense of fulfillment. Debbie Stevens Palmour was the person responsible for Christy and me being involved with Nancy Harmon. Debbie was the head of Voices of Worship Northeast Georgia and had been the piano accompanist for me at Steve's funeral. Later she resigned from her position as the worship leader at The River Community Church and Christy would take the position. We also moved into the church parsonage. Christy and I were now both worship leaders at different churches, but greatly fulfilled being involved in ministry.

Harvest Assembly

Harvest Assembly of God in Cleveland, Georgia, holds a special place in my heart for a number of reasons, but probably most of all because of Pastor Jimmy Sargent and his straightforward preaching and teaching from the Word of God. My favorite quote from him was about protecting the flock from wolves. When a man comes into a congregation and tries to seduce women or abuse them in some way, we call that a wolf among the sheep. Pastor Jimmy always said, "We don't allow wolves in here, we just knock them in the head." I still laugh at that every time I think about it, but in a realistic sense, he was one of the most vigilant men of God I had ever met as it relates to guarding the flock against deception and temptation. Hophni and Phinehas (Eli's two evil sons) in 1 Samuel 2:34 would not have stood a chance there.

One of the other things that I was truly blessed to do was to be a part of the band playing keyboards. I typically get someone else to play for me when I put together a band because there are so many who are so much better than me. Primarily, I am a singer. However, to have to read the music charts and play along with other musicians was truly refreshing. One Sunday morning when I had just left the platform and before taking my seat, a sister by the name of Ann Busby Fennell leaned over to me and said, "I don't usually do this kind of thing, but I've been praying for you, and I believe that the Lord would have me tell you that He will restore you in the ministry that He has called you to." Ann is the wife of Pastor Harrison Fennell, the former pastor of Harvest Assembly, and the love I felt from them both was always a wonderful, encouraging comfort. It was about a month or so later that Pastor Jimmy spoke very similar words to me before the whole congregation. I realized then that God had brought me to this church not only for me to be a blessing to the body there, but also that I would be encouraged by prophetic words. I would soon need them in ways I could not have imagined.

Mundy Mill Road

I was giving a student a ride to the University of North Georgia on Mundy Mill Road in Gainesville. I can't even remember what we were talking about, but as I was driving along, we both started laughing. I laughed so hard that I started to cough, and then I coughed so hard that I started to feel lightheaded. The next thing I remember was feeling the car bouncing on an uneven surface. I had blacked out and run off the side of the road and was now in the middle of an open field. As I drove off the field back to a side street, I knew that it was nothing short of a miracle I hadn't run off the road and hit one of the telephone poles lining that area of the road. God's hand was protecting me again.

The Voice

I auditioned for the singing competition television show *The Voice*, and on January 27, 2016, I received a letter letting me know I had made it through the first round and was being asked to the next phase of auditions. I was truly excited at this prospect, and I shared it with Christy immediately. As always, she was my biggest advocate and was delighted at this news. She immediately wanted to tell everybody she knew about it, but the confidentiality agreement that I signed restricted that. When I originally registered to audition back in December of 2015, I had received this message in an email from Tobin Hyman, a talent producer for the show.

Hi Mister Gaines,

My name is Tobin Hyman and I am a talent producer for NBC's "The Voice." I found in our database where you've registered to audition for us in Memphis on January 23. Thank you for adding the video links as you have a great voice. I'm well aware of your rich history in Christian/ Gospel music, as I am a preacher's kid and used to work in CCM. I would like to discuss you getting to skip the Open Call and come to an appointment audition in Memphis. Would January 26 work for you?

I replied to that email with a big yes, and in my subsequent telephone conversation with Tobin, he revealed he had worked with DC Talk and knew that I had sung background vocals on their *Free at Last* CD. I recounted to him that the recording session for that project was the most fun recording session I had ever been involved in. That day we recorded the vocals to the songs "Socially Acceptable," "Word to the Father," and "Love is a Verb." Here again, the amazing favor of God was manifest in this connection from the past. Though I didn't receive the call back for the next round of auditions, I see the hand of God in this as well. He foreknew things to come and just how difficult it would have been to be a part of *The Voice* with all that I would soon encounter.

Brasstown Bald

It was February 6, 2015, and in keeping with her philosophy of living intentionally and creating memories, Christy had planned a trip to Brasstown Bald, which is a part of the Blue Ridge Mountains range. With an elevation of 4783 feet above sea level, it is the highest point in the state of Georgia. It is a very popular tourist attraction and a perch from which you can see four states: Georgia, North Carolina, Tennessee, and South Carolina. At this time of year, it would have typically been covered with snow, but it was a clear and beautiful day.

As we sat in the theatre watching the video presentation about Brasstown Bald, my cell phone rang. It was my cousin Wanda Falden. Her news was stunning. She said that my cousin Tom (known as Dee) had passed away. He was the one who had led me to the Lord, the one I had walked with and talked for hours about the scriptures, the one who came and got me out of a house party in the neighborhood where I had no business being, the one who rebuked me when I had gone astray. Here at the highest point in Georgia was one of my lowest moments in life.

My cousin Dee had called me in the summer of 2001 to tell me that he had a stroke. I was shocked. He explained that his doctors believed it was associated with the open-heart surgery he had as a child. Around the year 2013, I received another call from him telling me he was in bad shape physically and that his doctor had told him he could die at any time. He also made a request that stunned me. He said, "If I die, please tell people that I was not a monster." I wailed on the phone.

Through my broken sobs, I asked, "How is it that you have lived your life as a Christian these forty-some years, and now you believe the summation of your life is that you were a monster?"

He told me about marital problems he was having. I have learned that a one-sided account of marital issues is never adequate to draw a conclusion of fault or blame, but one thing was for sure, I was talking to an obviously broken man.

In January of 2015, he called to tell me he had been diagnosed with a rare and aggressive form of cancer and that he was beginning chemotherapy. It was only about a couple of weeks, and he was gone. My Aunt Ruth, a younger sister of my mother who was like a mother to Dee, told me that he died of a broken heart. This one thing I know: Dee was the single greatest influence of my life as a Christian, of anyone on this earth. And for that I am grateful. The hand of God in my life was most apparent through my cousin Dee.

This is a Facebook post I shared to honor my cousin's passing:

Thomas Lewis Todd:
August 31, 1952 - February 6, 2015

"Empowered By His Scars"

It was his scars that first intrigued me about my first cousin, the first-born son of my mother's younger sister, Harriett. A suture scar in the middle of his chest, the remnant of open-heart surgery as an infant due to being born with a hole in his heart, and the other surgical scar on his forearm, the result of surgery to repair a compound fracture resulting from his death grip on the handlebars of his bicycle when struck by a car as a boy. It was those scars, the realization of his mortality, and his numerous near brushes with death that would fuel his gratitude for life and an understanding for why his life had been preserved. I was twelve years old when he first witnessed to me about Christ, and it was shortly after my own brush with death, having been struck by a car and nearly killed. I received what he had to say gladly, but I had no root, and withered quickly when he returned to Hampton, Virginia, after the summer stay.

What is it about having your cousins come and visit for the summer that was so amazing and fun? For me it would always end up with me hiding in the bathroom to cry when they left. Well, I'm crying now as I write because someone that I loved is gone. I'm not grieving as someone who has no hope, because I know that to be absent from the body is to be present with the Lord, but really I cry for myself and the fact that there is one less voice in my life that had been an anchor of encouragement. To me he was always "Dee." I can still hear his voice on the end of the phone a few days ago, saying, "Hey, Gaines."

It would be one year after his first attempt to convert me that at the corner of Corbin and Akron Street I would see him in a taxicab arriving to Richmond, my hometown, to attend VCU (Virginia Commonwealth University). My immediate thought was, "Oh no! I don't want to see him." The very sight of him reminded me of how far I had fallen, and his very presence would in the future steer me from a multitude of trouble. Like the time that he heard I was at a house party and came there to get me, or when I called myself "having a girlfriend" at 15. It was his voice that very rightly said, "She's leading you away from the Lord." He was one of those brave Christians who rebuked you because they really loved you. Yes, proximity is a must for successful discipleship. He was my first pastor—that's right, my 17-year-old cousin.

He related another one of his near-death experiences to me of being at Buckroe Beach in Hampton, Virginia, and wading in safe, warm summer waters when a girl around his age encouraged him to venture out away from the shore. What he didn't know was that she was treading water and that he was only feet away from a bottom drop off. Yep, he sank like a rock. He told me that he still doesn't know how he got back to shore, but when he got back to the beach, he kissed the sand. That always stuck with me.

Our nightly prayers on the stone benches that lined the back entry of John Marshall High School, along with our cousin Charles Johnson and my younger brother Jonathan, was where we would call out the names of every single person in our family before God. Those prayers produced great fruit! (That's a lot of people. There were 33 first cousins alone.) Now, as I look at my life with all of its ups and downs, I am eternally grateful that God sent a teenager from Hampton, Virginia, to Richmond, Virginia, to start a family revival that is still bearing fruit. Everyone I've touched with the gospel is a star in his crown.

Sarah Gaines, Karen Todd, Thomas "Dee" Todd,
Billy Gaines, April Blue Taylor

Me, my cousin Wanda
Falden, and Sarah.

The Greatest Challenge Ever

Christy and I had been married for two years, had moved to a different home, and were happy with the life God had blessed us with. We were both delighted to be involved in ministry and to be working as worship leaders. By this time I was on the worship team and playing keyboards with the band at Harvest Assembly of God in Cleveland, Georgia. On April 20, 2017, Christy and I drove to Greenville, South Carolina, for me to appear on the *Nite Line Show* with Mary Sloan and her daughter, Toni Sloan Suchka. The show was great, and this was by far our most enjoyable trip together ever. That happy day would soon be overshadowed by what would happen exactly one week later on Thursday, April 27, 2017.

Christy was filming at WATC TV 57 with Debbie Palmour and The Voices of Worship Northeast Georgia but had left early and returned home because she wasn't feeling well. The next morning, she couldn't make it to the filming at all because her abdomen was in so much pain. That following morning we decided to go to the emergency room, where Christy had an ultrasound scan of her abdomen. While I was waiting in the emergency room with Christy, my daughter Rachel called me and told me that Sarah had been diagnosed with terminal lung cancer. Not long after that, the doctors told us there was a mass in Christy's pancreas and they would need to do a biopsy. It was an unbelievably difficult day. Christy's biopsy would show that she had an inoperable malignant tumor in her pancreas, which was devastating news for everybody. She would begin chemotherapy shortly after that. I was very fortunate that a friend of mine gave me a whole month's salary so I could be by Christy's side for the first month of her treatment.

One of the greatest lessons I learned in the middle of all this heartbreak was that we need to worship the Lord even with wounded and broken hearts. One of the sweetest moments we had together was on one of our countless trips to the hospital. Christy was lying down in the back seat, and as she often did, she asked me to pray and sing. While I was driving along singing and worshiping, I felt the gentlest, warm hand on the back of my head. I lost it and wept because with all the pain that she was going through, Christy still found the strength to lift her hand to make such a loving gesture. But that was Christy, the sweetest, most affectionate, most kind, most loving and selfless person I had ever met. She was truly a peacekeeper; she always wanted everyone to love one another.

To watch this wonderful woman that I loved so deeply going through all of this suffering was an absolute nightmare, but I still saw the hand of God in the love and care and help that was poured out on Christy. The church paid her weekly the entire time she was sick, even when she couldn't make it to church. Other family members gave her total living expenses for a six-month period. Her friends were by her side, caring for her and loving her: Liz Allman, Cheryl Martin Wright, Dena Torres-Cantu, Heidi Brooks Smith, Nyoka Brooks. A special comfort to her were her sisters Linda Greene and Jelly Valimont, and her mother Olene Jordan. Nancy Harmon called to pray for Christy. Probably the most notable thing that happened was a call that I got from Sarah asking to speak to Christy. She told Christy that she didn't hold anything against her, which brought peace to all of us.

Sorrow

It was the morning of January 25, 2018, that I got the call from Christy's sister Jelly telling me I needed to come. Christy was now in hospice care at her mother's home. I was at home that morning, but Jelly was at her mother's with Christy, along with a hospice nurse. I didn't ask any questions because I knew what this call meant. When I arrived and went into the room and saw the lifeless body of my wife lying there, it was as if I had lost everything. I realized in that moment I was in the middle of one of my most dreaded fears, and yet the overwhelming sense of loss could not displace my love and my trust in my Savior.

The day of the funeral I woke up with such a heaviness on me that I felt like I couldn't even get out of bed, and when I arrived at the chapel, it was even worse. I would have to say that the grief was the worst I'd ever experienced. Not long after that, though, when we went into the sanctuary for the ceremony, the singing started and something supernatural happened. As I began to sing along with them and worship, the knowledge of the hope of the resurrection and of eternal life flooded my spirit, and I can truly say that I had joy in the midst of my grief. And Christy's last words to me the night before she died have replayed in my mind countless times, "I feel better now that you prayed." I also kept in my mind the words she said to me a week before she died that you would have to hear to fully understand, "I love you so much." I cannot begin to tell you the comfort that I have received by rehearsing those moments in my mind. It is one thing to be delivered from trouble and recognize the hand of God, but now I was experiencing the hand of God as a comfort in my sorrow.

Loss of a Gift

One of the stories in the Bible that always troubled me was that of Jacob, and how his wife Rachel, whom he had waited for so long and labored so intensely for, had been defrauded by her father. After Jacob finally received her, she died in childbirth after bearing her son Benjamin. There was a sense of dread every time I read that story, as well as a deep sense of fear. I hoped nothing like that would ever happen to me.

One of the sweetest stories I've ever heard was what Mrs. Olene Jordan, Christy's mother, shared with me. She had two children, and she hadn't been able to get pregnant for a number of years, and yet she prayed continually that God would give her another child. So when she became pregnant, she was overjoyed at her answered prayer. She shared with me that she was so overjoyed while she was carrying Christy, that even though she had morning sickness, she was throwing up and laughing at the same time because she was so happy to be pregnant. Christy was her treasured and prayed for gift from God, and she was adored by her parents and by her sisters also.

I wish upon no one the grief of losing a marriage. I know that in some circumstances people would consider getting out of a marriage or being divorced to be a relief from misery or from trouble. I can't speak for Sarah, but for me it was the worst grief that I had experienced in my life up to that point. For years I cried every single day, and for some reason it was while I was washing dishes. I don't know whether it was the warm water on my hands or some other trigger that caused it, but there I was every day, my hands in warm water, crying like a baby. So when Christy came into my life, she was a gift to me and a redemption of my grief over my loss of Sarah. I was a gift to her also in the midst of her grief for her loss of Steve. I couldn't help but think about Jacob and his loss of his wife Rachel as I looked at my present situation of losing Christy to cancer. The only remedy for horrible grief was gratitude for the time that I had her as my wife.

God's Goodness and Mercy

Nashville 2018

After Christy's death, I moved back to Franklin, Tennessee. In His goodness and mercy, God had given me two of the most wonderful friends anyone could ever have, Marcus and Tina Wilson, who had already for years allowed me to stay in their home when I traveled between Gainesville and Nashville. Now they allowed me to have a place to live and grieve and heal. In April of that year, I moved to Goodlettsville, just north of Nashville, to be near my daughter Rachel, her husband Brian, and my grandkids Olivia and Briley. I found great comfort being near them. Still grieving deeply, I realized it was not a grief of hopelessness that I was going through, but rather the grief of enormous loss of someone that your life revolved around.

Mary Sloan Surprise

I had met Mary Sloan during the first taping of Nancy Harmon's *Jesus Connection* at WTAC TV 57 in Norcross, Georgia. When she stepped out to sing and took the microphone, I immediately recognized her genuine spirit, and I loved her voice and her songs. As I mentioned earlier, she would invite me to sing on her *Nite Line* program. It was July 9 that I received an email from Mary about her new album she was finishing, with an attachment of two of the songs for me to review with the possibility of me singing on one or both of them. I loved the songs and was eager to be a part of this project. I recorded a duet with Mary Sloan entitled "I Kept My Praise."

Sarah

On Thursday, September 20, 2018, I received a text from Rachel letting me know that Sarah had just been taken in for surgery at Vanderbilt Medical Center. She asked me to bring food from one of Sarah's favorite restaurants for her to eat after she came out of surgery. When I arrived with the food, Sarah was still unconscious and the doctors and nurses were still working with her. I left that day without seeing her, but I would visit and pray for Sarah consistently. It was in those visits that I was reminded that the love of God and His kingdom supersedes all levels of relationships, whether friendships or marriages, and that the bond that we have as brothers and sisters in Christ is eternal. In heaven, Jesus says we will not marry or be given in marriage, but we will be like the angels. He also says that the former things will not be remembered in the overall scheme of things. Only the eternal aspects of our life and our existence are what really matter in the end. We are eternal beings, and all the events, circumstances, pains, and ups and downs of life will have no relevance in eternity.

Kathie Lee Gifford

As I mentioned earlier, back in 1987 I had done some painting at Calico Corners store in Green Hills for a sound engineer named Chris McCollum. I had worked with Chris recording at Great Circle Sound, the recording studio in the Benson Music Company building. I would check with him periodically throughout the years to see if he had any jobs going on for me to earn some extra money. Back in the summer of 2016, I was scheduled to travel from Gainesville to Nashville for a few days, so

I contacted Chris to see if he had any work I could do. He told me that he didn't have any jobs going on, but that his brother Greg was the COO of a new company called Takl and that I should check it out. I did so and signed up to be a provider for Takl. Takl was an app-driven, on-demand service request platform. I referred to it as being an Uber for any kind of job that you needed to be tackled. My particular skill set with this company was what I would call mechanical, electrical, installation and assembly. My specialty was the installation of flat screen televisions, ceiling fans, and light fixtures.

It was Saturday, October 27, 2018. I had been visiting Sarah at Vanderbilt Hospital when I received a text message from Greg McCollum asking me to do a job for his wife Angie down in Franklin. My initial thought was to wonder why he wanted me to do a job for his wife. You can imagine my trepidation, doing a job for the wife of the COO of this company! If I performed a job for a regular customer and there was something they were not pleased with, that complaint would be lodged at a lower level of management and be resolved there. But if something were to go wrong with this job, the complaint would be lodged directly to the COO from his wife. Yikes. However, I took the job and headed down to Franklin from Vanderbilt Hospital in Nashville.

When I arrived, I was greeted by Angie, and the first thing she said was, "I'm so glad to meet you! Greg has told me all about you, and that you are the number one provider for the company. That's why he chose you for this job." I was absolutely shocked to learn that I was the number one provider for the company, and said so to Angie. That's when she let me know this job was not for her but for one of her clients.

We entered a beautiful brownstone through the lower level, got on the elevator, and went up to the second floor. When we stepped off the elevator, the first thing I thought to myself was that this place was beautiful. The next thing I noticed was a lovely, black baby grand piano sitting in the middle of this completely empty room with gorgeous hardwood floors. Angie had exited the elevator ahead of me, and as I stood there in amazement at the beauty of this place and that piano, she said, "Billy, I would like to introduce you to my client, Kathie." As she gestured to my left, I turned, and there was Kathie Lee Gifford standing there with arms crossed, smiling. It was a jaw-dropping moment, and I was absolutely shocked. After Angie introduced us by first names, she asked me what my last name was. When I answered Gaines, Angie was surprised.

"Billy Gaines, as in Billy and Sarah Gaines?" she asked. Yes that's me.

"Oh, my goodness, I love your music, and I've listened to you for years."

The next thing out of Angie's mouth was the question, "Don't you play piano?" Within minutes, I was sitting at that piano playing, then singing. Then Kathie Lee Gifford joined in with me to sing worship songs together. Before I knew it, Kathie Lee was running back and forth to her office to grab lyrics to songs she had written and was placing them in front of me to see if I could quickly put music to them. Well, I had to let her know I wasn't that fast of a writer. After some time of singing and worshipping together, I finally got to work hanging mirrors in the hallway of her bottom entryway. Later on, just before it was time for us to eat, I was able to talk to Kathie Lee and relate my story to her about Sarah presently being in the hospital with lung cancer and Christy's having died of pancreatic cancer January 25 of that year.

A number of the members of the McCollum family arrived with pizza, and because there were no chairs in this beautiful condominium, everyone sat on the floor to eat. Kathie Lee then spoke up and said, "We're gonna have Billy sing for us." So I sat there and did what I would have to characterize as a mini concert. When I finished the song "Other Side of this Trial," I could see that Kathie Lee was moved. She asked me if I'd written the song, and I said yes. She said she could tell. "How are you doing with all of this?" she asked, and before I could answer, she answered me and said, "I know you're sad and you're lonely, aren't you?" I said yes, I am. Then she said, "Well, Billy came here to hang pictures, but the real reason that he came here was for us to pray over him." She called for everyone to gather around me and just lay hands on me. One of the most memorable things about that moment was when Kathie Lee placed her hands on my head to pray for me, and just how warm her hands were. The best way I can describe that moment of those hands being on me praying for me was that it was as if someone was pouring liquid love all over me.

I became Kathie Lee's primary provider from Takl for the next year. It seemed that every time I came over, she was playing me a new song she had written. I remember so well her playing some of the songs that were a part of her movie *Then Came You*. One day stands out in particular, though. She explained to me that she and Nicole C. Mullen had written a song, "The God Who Sees," that she intended for Danny Gokey to record, but when he heard the song, he said this song is for Nicole to record. She played the song, and I stood there and wept like a baby. She placed her arm around me, and with her other hand she pointed at me to indicate that this song was for me. Truly it was for me, and every time I hear it now, I still tear up.

More Work to Takl

It was on October 17, 2019, that Angie contacted me once again and told me Kathie Lee had some more work for me, but that what she really wanted to do was talk to me about music. When I arrived, Kathie Lee told me she had been praying for me and she believed God wanted me to get back into music more seriously. She then explained she had a role she wanted me to audition for. Another artist had already been offered the role and she

was waiting to hear from him. She let me know that if that artist came through, the song would be his, but I should prepare anyway just in case. Well, that artist did come through, but she told me not to worry, she had another role for me to audition for. This role was for the part of Moses. I auditioned on Friday, October 25. Michelle Margiotta, whom we refer to affectionately as Moosh, did the orchestra arrangements and was there to accompany me for my audition. The song was "The God of the How and When." When I finished my audition, Kathie Lee approached me and said very emphatically, "You. Are. Moses."

In November I recorded the vocals at Sal Oliveri's studio. I was in for a big surprise because I learned just how much of an amazing vocal producer Kathie Lee is. She knew exactly what she wanted, and she even literally directed me on some of the cutoffs on the notes and the phrasing of the song. On Monday, December 2, 2019, I had the wonderful pleasure and privilege of being at Ocean Way Studio in Nashville to hear the orchestra record this song. It was an amazing day, to say the least. While we were eating lunch, Kathie Lee reminded me that in conjunction with this recording, we would actually be filming this song in the Holy Land in Israel. Unfortunately, COVID set in, and there were repeated delays that kept pushing the filming back further and further. As an alternative, they chose to scout out locations in the United States that were similar in terrain and appearance to the Holy Land.

Sarah's Final Days

I would have to say that Sarah was blessed with some of the most loving, dedicated friends anyone could ever hope for, many who came from out of state to visit and help care for her. One visitor that had a very special place in her heart was our son Nathan, whom she had not seen for about three years. He lives in Los Angeles and doesn't come to Nashville often. She was overjoyed to see him.

On Thursday, January 17, 2019, I received a call from my son Jason, who was now going by the name Michael. The doctors had called all of the family to come to the hospital. As I walked down the hospital hallway, I saw my niece Natasha, my sister Barbara's daughter, from a distance. As I neared, I saw tears in her eyes, and she softly uttered the words, "She's gone." Sarah had been ushered into eternity. I sat on the additional bed in her room and wept. Not long after that, Rachel and Brian arrived, and as Rachel wept over her mother, I heard a sound in her weeping that I had not heard since she was a little girl. Then in the midst of this grief and weeping emerged the sweetest utterance of worship I have ever witnessed. Rachel's voice broke through all her grief and anguish and began singing and worshiping God. It was in that moment I was reminded just how much God valued worship from a wounded heart.

Worship from A Wounded Heart
VERSE 1

Here in this season of my anguish, loss, and pain
When all of my humanness would lead me to complain
I am resolved that I will glorify Your name,

Evermore, come what may
Lingering questions go unanswered up to now
Still at your throne of grace I trustingly will bow
Not looking back in doubt, my hand is to the plow
Here I am, right now

CHORUS

Lord, I worship you right now
Lord you hold the answer to the when, the why, or how
Lord, I worship you right now
My offering, worship from a wounded heart

VERSE 2

Broken and contrite hearts, I know you won't despise
Faith in the face of pain is precious in your eyes
Your loving ears are always open to my cries
Here I am right now
I have a song that cannot wait for answered prayers
Nor for the remedy of all of my life's cares
My declaration I must utter unaware
Of just how, but for now

CHORUS

Lord, I worship you right now
Lord you hold the answer to the when, the why, or how
Lord, I worship you right now
My offering, worship from a wounded heart

BRIDGE

Though I sing this song with a broken heart, choking back the tears
The sweetest sound that I can make has fallen on Your ears
Though the heavens and earth may pass way, Lord, You remain the same
My hope still stands, my faith still holds, to the power of your name

Reconnection

I was contacted by Brian Mason on February 26, 2019. Brian had a Sunday morning radio show years ago that Sarah and I had been on a number of times. He was reaching out to me to invite me to a prayer group comically called the old CCM (Contemporary Christian Music) Dudes. He assured me that it was a term of endearment! I was really glad to hear from him, and I was looking forward to the meeting. On Wednesday, March 20, 2019, we met at the Sportsman's Lodge in Cool Springs. When I arrived, I saw guys I hadn't seen in years, including Gary Chapman, Phil Keaggy, Eddie DeGarmo, Nathan DiGesare, and Bruce Carroll. I sensed this was going to be a time of destiny, and I was right. Bruce Carroll sat next to me and asked what I was doing for the rest of the day. I told him that I didn't have any plans. He invited me to come to the Music City Fathers retreat meeting. A few minutes after that, he turned to me and said, "I believe this is destiny, from the Lord." I told him I knew the moment that he asked me what I had planned for the rest of the day, that it was destiny.

When I arrived at the retreat later that day, I soon saw John G. Elliott, my songwriting collaborator and the producer of our first album. It had been more than twenty years since I had seen John, and both of us were overjoyed to see each other. We went on a walk for a couple of miles and had a great conversation, catching up on what was going on in each other's lives. I sang "You are Faithful" during the evening session while John accompanied me on piano. It was a wonderful time of ministry, with Bruce Carroll, Bob Bennett, Rob Frazier, and others singing and playing. At one point, all of the brothers gathered around me, laid hands on me, and prayed for me, speaking words of encouragement over me. I'm now a part of the monthly Old CCM Dudes prayer meeting, and it is so good to be reconnected.

Christy's Answered Prayers

The date was Friday March 22, 2019, when I received a call from Reagan Meeks, Christy's youngest son. He wanted to tell me about the mission trip to Puerto Rico he had gone on with his church, Griffin First Assembly of God in Griffin, Georgia. My heart was flooded with joy to hear they had done six chapel services at one of the schools, ministered at ten different nursing homes and an orphanage, and that he personally had preached the gospel for at least one of the services. All of this was under the guidance of his uncle, Pastor Randy Valimont, Christy's brother-in-law. I only wished Christy could have been alive to hear it and that I could have seen the look on her face as she witnessed this manifestation of her answered prayers for her children.

A Simpler Time

It was Sunday June 16, 2019, Father's Day. I had driven from Nashville to Urbana, Virginia, that previous Thursday to stay with Brian and Audrey Hingley. My primary purpose for this trip was for Audrey to help me finish my book and add additional information. I had initially contacted her to help me write this book by interviewing me,

Pastor Bill Smalt who played guitar for Living Sacrifice, Brian and Audrey Hingley, and me

and as time went on and as she prayed about it, I sensed the Lord leading me to just simply start writing. It was amazing that the more I wrote, the more I remembered, and I had a real sense that the Holy Spirit was bringing all these things back to my memory. Before long, I had written so much that I was amazed, and I almost felt like if I hadn't lived these events, they would seem like fiction. But I knew in my spirit Audrey was the one to help me finish this book.

Brian and Audrey Hingley will always hold a very special place in my heart. To begin with, I have known them since I was fourteen. I met them in 1970 at the Open Doorway Coffeehouse before they were married. When I was sixteen, I attended their wedding in 1972. Their wedding was the very first inspiration I had to desire a marriage deeply dedicated and rooted in Christ. Sarah and I would also later see Brian and Audrey in 1978 at the Christian Music Festival, Fishnet, in Front Royal, Virginia. After we moved from Hampton to Richmond in October of 1980, Audrey booked us to sing at Aslan's, a Christian music venue in Shockoe Slip in downtown Richmond. Amazingly, Tess Erwin, who was our publicist at Benson Records, would later hire Audrey to write press releases for us.

I can't begin to tell you just how at home I felt there with Brian and Audrey. It was as if I had gone back in time and was reliving the warmth and comfort of early days of the Jesus Movement and coffeehouse. What intensified this sentiment was a video Audrey shared about the Jesus Movement. I had never seen it before, and I tear up just thinking about it now. It brought back so many precious memories of a simpler time, when a kid with an afro could show up at a coffeehouse in the Fan District of Richmond and become a part of what some would call Christian hippies. What a wonderful time, long before I knew anything about the recording industry, song positions on radio charts, managers, agents, or technical riders for appearance contracts. It was a time when all I knew was that God had called me to minister the gospel through music. Pure and simple.

Amazingly, while I was sitting there absorbed in this trip down memory lane, I got a notification from Facebook. It was the sweetest Father's Day tribute from my daughter Rachel that any father could ever imagine. I turned to Brian and Audrey and read the tribute and told them that this tribute Rachel wrote to me was a fulfillment of a prophecy I had received. What a day! It was as if the Lord had decided to give me a bath of love, comfort, and joy. Truthfully, that day was a day of renewal for me. And though this book is limited by the time frame in which it was finished, I know God is not finished with me. I believe with all of my heart that He is a rewarder of those who diligently seek Him and that He will complete that which concerns me and will not forsake (me) the works of his hands (Psalm 138:8).

More Prophetic Utterances

There were a number of amazing things that happened during the wait time after I recorded the song in Kathie Lee's movie, *The Way*. They added further evidence of God's mighty hand working in my life and on my behalf because of the connections that had been made through Kathie Lee Gifford. Kathie Lee invited me to a meeting on Sunday, January 19, 2020, where Rabbi Jason Sobel would be speaking. The meeting was held at Tim and Dianna Akers' home in Franklin, Tennessee. I really didn't know what to expect or even what the meeting was all about, and it was my first time being exposed to Rabbi Jason Sobel. Of all the things that he could have spoken on that night, he spoke on the concept of the hidden hand of God. He was relating the story of Esther, her cousin Mordecai, and Haman, and how—through a series of events—God moved on the Jews' behalf to save them from Haman's plan to kill them. It was a wonderful and inspiring message. Afterward, as I was enjoying the food and fellowship, I finally got to meet Rabbi Jason. Later, after we spoke, I noticed he seemed to be pacing back and forth near me, as if he were contemplating something. He then turned to me and said, "I have a word for you. The Lord has shown me that you are like a fine top-shelf wine that has been aged, and it's time for you to be taken off the shelf and be poured out and served to others." I was stunned, to put it plainly. On two separate occasions that same evening, he would say to me, "Remember, off the shelf," as if to reiterate the urgency of this directive.

This prophetic utterance was fulfilled in the most amazing way. It was August 29, 2019, that I had recorded the song "I Kept My Praise" with Mary Sloan on her new CD. It was Mary Sloan who introduced me to Marcia Lucas, who was filming the movie *A Breath Away from a Wonderful Life*. Marcia wanted me to play the role of a villain, a driver, and a corpse in her film. Filming took place in Pigeon Forge, Tennessee, in September of 2020. I recorded the song "Walking Down Wine Street" as a duet with Marcia for the soundtrack of the same movie, as well as "I am Christmas." As of today, Marcia's movie is still in post-production.

Later that year, Tami Jones Andrews asked me to record three duets on her Christmas CD, *Together Apart*: "This Christmas," "Mary Did You Know," and a Christmas version of "From a Distance." We also filmed the video of those three songs. I was beginning to get off the shelf.

Playing Moses

The next fulfillment of that prophecy was finally being able to film the part of Moses. In October of 2020, I flew to Salt Lake City, Utah, where Kathie Lee and her team had chosen Antelope Island State Park as the site to film my portion of the movie *The Way*. I played the character of Moses, singing "The God of the How and When." That evening after the filming, we met back at the hotel for dinner together. Aaron Greene, the producer, Christine Gardner, Kathie Lee's assistant, Kathie Lee and I were there. I was thanking Kathie Lee profusely for choosing me to be a part of this wonderful movie. Her reply to me was, "I didn't choose you; God chose you. I just asked him to show me whom He had chosen." The movie was finally released in theaters on September 1, 2022, and as of December 2 is being streamed on the Pure Flix platform.

I played the part of Moses in Kathie Lee's movie because of a relationship with Chris McCollum from thirty years before. I learned from this just how much of an amazing long-term planner God is. He truly does go before us. He is already in our future, He creates the circumstances,

and He brings together all the players. God puts together all the elements, the moving parts, and all the people who are designated to be involved in the story of our lives. He orchestrates it all so beautifully and with such precision that we could not even begin to understand or imagine. This is simply further evidence of just how great our Heavenly Father is. We can put our trust in Him because He not only sees the right now, He sees into our future, and He is a perpetual, masterful designer, director, and planner, who has promised us that as we submit ourselves to Him, trusting Him with all of our hearts and leaning not on our own understanding, He will indeed direct our steps.

Off the Shelf

The year 2021 was further evidence of me being poured out in a new way. In April I recorded the song "Great, Great King," produced by Sal Oliveri and written by Sal, Barbara Ann Jeter, and Julie Butler Smith. In June I recorded "I Wanna Be Holding You" as a duet with Dawn Rix for her country radio single, and in July I recorded the songs "That's How Much He Loves Us," and "Midnight Praise," as duets on B. J. Pons CD. At one point, I remember thinking to myself that I must be the guy to record duets with this year!

I also filmed the live performance of "Sunday's On The Way," and "Hunger For Holiness" for the Carman tribute on TBN in August of that year.

The next amazing thing to happen was on March 25 of 2022, when I recorded the song "There Will Come a Day." It was written by Thornton Douglas Cline and Lacey Carpenter. The song went to number one on the European Independent Artist charts. It was astonishing to me that the same songwriter who co-wrote "Love Is The Reason" that landed us our first contract with the Benson Company had now asked me to record another song all these years later. This song jump-started my popularity again and brought increased exposure to my music worldwide. It also opened many new doors for me, including being played on WHIN Radio by Jeff Shannon Hawkins in Hendersonville, which led to his wife Kathleen, who was president of the Hendersonville Chamber of Commerce, choosing me to perform this song for the Hendersonville Freedom Fest on July 3rd of that year.

There were more amazing connections. In November of 2022, I was attending an event in Hendersonville when a lady by the name of Marie Cosgrove approached me and asked me to be involved in a Christmas program she was planning that was similar to the Trans-Siberian Orchestra Christmas program. It was truly amazing that the Lord was surely bringing to pass His word in my life.

The Way Movie Premiere Release

It was June 20, 2022. The filming of the movie, post-production, editing, and color correction were all done now, and we would finally get to see the finished product. You can imagine what a great sense of joy and satisfaction I had when I received this email from Christine Gardner, Kathie Lee's assistant and co-producer of the movie:

> *Billy,*
>
> *I wanted to make sure you knew that it looks like* THE WAY *will be released in theaters on September 1st. It's a Fathom release, which means it will be in theaters for one night only. We are waiting to hear the exact number of theaters, but it looks like over 700 nationwide!*
>
> *Kathie will be having a "red carpet" event at a local theater TBD so please keep the date marked on your calendar. We need Moses in attendance!*
>
> *Billy Gaither will then release a CD of the music and a DVD of the whole film. So exciting!*
>
> *We're so grateful you were a part of this project, Billy. We're hoping it blesses so many!*

The night of the Premiere was truly a wonderful and momentous occasion. It took place at the historic Franklin Theater, in Franklin, Tennessee. Quite frankly, being in a movie was something I never even imagined myself doing! It was surreal to sit in that theater and to see all of the cast members up on the big screen, including Matt Bauer as Abraham, Julie Roberts as Sarah, me as Moses, Larry Gatlin as Joshua, Nicole C. Mullen as Hagar, Danny Gokey as himself, Kathy Troccoli as the woman at the well, Chuck Harmony as the demoniac, BeBe Winans as the prodigal son's father, Jimmy Allen as the prodigal son, and Claude Kelly as the prodigal son's older brother. The red-carpet event was another joyous experience as we took photos and did interviews with the press. The after-party was held at the American Tap House Restaurant just a few blocks down the street, where great food, more celebration, congratulations, and conversation continued. I was blessed to be part of this project!

Remembering Family

Mary Kathryn Gaines

My sister, Mary Kathryn Gaines, was one of the greatest helps and contributors to my and Sarah's ministry. She was eighteen years older than me, and though I was her baby brother, it was as if I were her baby also, as she assisted my mother in caring for me. She would laugh often and give accounts of the humor of my mispronunciation of certain words.

I learned how to drive very early; my father and my older siblings would succumb to my constant begging them to let me drive. My brother Herman had an old car in his yard with a three-speed manual shift on the steering column. I remember practicing shifting gears and working the clutch, just dreaming of driving a stick shift someday. Well, that day came, and my sister Mary Kathryn had given me the real-time opportunity of learning how to drive her 1968 Buick Skylark with a three-speed stick on the steering column. She was so confident in my driving ability that she allowed me to take the car on a drive by myself. I was delighted and drove to the corner of Akron and John Street, made a left turn and went down to Jasper Avenue, made another left and drove to the corner of Jasper Avenue and Old Brook Road. I turned around in the John Marshall High School parking lot, then headed back down Jasper Avenue.

Now, Jasper Avenue was what we in Washington Park called the back road. It was notorious as a road where you could "open up a car." Translation: drive like you're driving a dragster. There was nothing like the sound and g-force of a Buick big block 455-cubic-inch engine with a Holley four-barrel carburetor feeding fuel to it. I was in muscle car heaven—until I downshifted to first gear going too fast and tore some of the teeth out of the rear end ring gear. I felt horrible. I was horrified to have to face my sister with the obvious halting and lurching motion and audible clunk of that rear end. Amazingly, she didn't speak a single chastising word. In 1978, when she allowed me to drive her new Buick Electra from Richmond to Florida, she was obviously one forgiving and trusting soul.

It was in 1985 after the birth of our son Nathan that she came from Richmond to Nashville to live with us and to help Sarah with our kids while we recorded our first record. She also traveled with us on the road as we toured the U.S. and Canada and was with us as we ministered on a number of cruises to Cancun, Mexico, and Puerto Rico. Apart from that, she was an amazing singer and worship leader in her own right. I had hoped she would record her own album and be signed to Benson Records. I told Dan Cleary about her, played one of her demos, and even set up a meeting between the two of them. I was truly excited when Dan Cleary came to our home to meet with her and talked to her about offering her a recording contract. Ultimately, though, she had been asked to move to Atlanta, Georgia, to work as an administrative assistant for Pastor Wellington Boone, and she felt that was more in line with God's will and purpose for her life.

On March 3, 1988, it was her voice on the other end of the phone informing me that my mother had passed away. I couldn't have imagined that it would only be nine years later, on October 5, 1999, that she would pass away also. In a letter from Wellington Boone that he sent to be read at Mary Kathryn's memorial service, he acknowledged that out of all the people who had followed him to Atlanta in the planting of the new church, Mary Kathryn was the only one he had commissioned to work for him. Once again, it is one more situation that I can only respond with gratitude in the face of grief and still focus on all the good, love, and sacrifice that she brought to so many in her lifetime. In all these things I still see the hand of God.

Jane Gaines Carey

My sister Jane was the third child born to my parents and what I called the baby of the first set of three kids that my mom and dad had. There was an unexplainable thirteen-year gap between the birth of Jane and my sister Barbara. My mother explained it this way: she went to her doctor and he told her that her womb was somehow twisted. He straightened it out, and in my parents' late thirties, there was an almost staircase procession of three more children. My brother and I were Irish twins, only sixteen months apart. When I was born, my brother Herman was twenty years old, enlisted in the Air Force and stationed in Africa. He didn't see me until I was one year old.

My sister Jane had grown up very ill with asthma and missed a lot of school. One of the most bizarre accounts of her illness was that the doctors had actually prescribed menthol cigarettes as a treatment for her asthma. Can you imagine that, a child smoking prescribed menthol cigarettes? She was also severely scratched by a cat as a little girl, which is amazing considering the fact that many years later she had a cat as a pet when she lived on Cheatwood Avenue in Richmond. That was when we discovered Sarah was allergic to cats. She was holding the cat during a prayer meeting at Jane's house when I observed her eyelids begin to swell.

My sister Jane would play a very important part in my musical development. All of the older siblings would play a role in my musical development. My brother Herman introduced me to the music of Sam Cooke, especially "A Change is Gonna Come," "Another Saturday Night," "The Tennessee Waltz," and the obscure but beautiful "When Shadows Fall." From my sister Barbara it was the 45 singles she would bring home: "Close to You" by the Carpenters and "Whiter Shade of Pale" by Procol

Harum. Then the string of Stevie Wonder albums. But it was my sister Jane's Roberta Flack and Donny Hathaway album that changed my musical life. There was something amazingly familial about Roberta and Donny's voices; I could hear similarities of Roberta's tone in my sister Mary Kathryn. I would honestly have to say that if it wasn't for hearing Donny Hathaway sing, I likely would have never chosen to pursue singing. I would have had the ability to sing but not the inspiration.

On a more comical note, it was a wonderful thing as a teenager with an afro to have sisters and other female relatives and friends do three things: scratch your dandruff, plait your hair, and grease your scalp. My preference was the blue Afro Sheen. On one occasion, my sister Jane had scratched my dandruff, I had shampooed my hair, and she suggested that she would rub some Vitalis in my hair. What neither of us knew or considered was that Vitalis contained alcohol and that the rawness of my scalp after her scratching my dandruff and that alcohol would not go well together. She poured it on and began to rub it in, and when the pain hit me, I dropped to the floor, writhing and rolling around. The absolute horror on her face and the tears that were beginning to well up in her eyes were an obvious indicator of her tender and merciful heart. All she could do was stand there and say, "I'm sorry, baby."

Yep, that was the endearing term I would always hear on the other end of the telephone when she would call me. "Hi, baby." And it was that same voice I would hear from weekly for decades. She called me every day after Christy's death to see how I was doing. It was unimaginable that on December 18, 2018, roughly eleven months after Christy's death and one month before Sarah's death, that she would pass away. It truly was a season of compounded grief. Once again, I am determined to extract the good from the grief and focus on the eternal and the fact that in all these things, I still see the hand of God.

Crowning Moments

Bearing Burdens

I learned an important lesson recently from a neighbor. I was on a ladder changing a lightbulb in front of my door in the breezeway where I live. My next-door neighbor came by and said to me, "I don't mean to embarrass you, but I've heard you singing and playing piano for the last few years, and I want you to know that your singing and playing got me through the darkest time of my life."

I was absolutely stunned. That was the first time I had ever spoken to that neighbor, and come to find out, he had lost his mother, and the last few years had been sad and painful for him. It showed me we just don't know what burdens others are bearing or the pain they are enduring. We can't always judge by appearances. He was actually moving out that day, and I knew God had appointed me to be on that ladder at that exact moment so I could know He had blessed my neighbor through me.

Tuesday, July 25, 2023

One of the challenges of ending this book is figuring out a cut-off point. With so many things on the horizon, I feel like I'm still right in the middle of so many present-day interventions of God's hand. It makes it difficult to say "enough said" for the moment. I realized that instead of a period, I needed to put a comma. This story is far from over! As a matter of fact, this story is inevitably perpetual because as long as we have breath, we know that our heavenly Father will be working on our behalf, giving us one new reason after another to glorify His name.

On Monday, July 24, I visited my daughter Rachel, her husband Brian, and my grandkids Olivia and Briley. After loving embraces and greetings from Rachel and the kids, I looked into the den and found Brian folding clothes.  This scene was so consistent with him as a person, a loving servant who cares for his family and will do whatever he can for them. It exemplified the process of modeling a servant's heart for his children to follow.

As I approached to embrace him, I offered an apology for missing his sermon the day before at church. At that moment Rachel chimed in, "Don't worry, you will have many more chances to hear his sermons." What I didn't know is that just a few days before, his father, Pastor Horace Hockett of Born Again Church in Nashville, had reiterated to him it was time to assume his role as senior pastor of the church. Well, you can imagine my heart leaped for joy! I was now seeing the product of the labor of Brian's parents, Horace and Kiwanis Hockett, who raised him in the ways of the Lord, and my and Sarah's labors raising our daughter Rachel to walk in the ways of the Lord, and it all resulted in this convergence of ministry through their lives. This truly was a crowning moment.

At whatever stage you find yourself while reading this book, whatever age, I believe that there's a universal truth that gratitude is the fuel of miraculous intervention, and scripture bears witness to that. Remember that your relevance in the eyes of God is not determined by your popularity in the eyes of men. We must be mindful of and purposely remember the things that God has done in our lives. They are the evidence of His presence, His power, and His very existence. If the Israelites who came out of Egypt had simply recounted all the wonderful things that God had done, they would have seen that the wilderness they were in was God's will for them. And in light of that, they should have trusted Him in the wilderness, remembering He was the same God who brought them out of slavery in Egypt.

I would like to encourage you to take a closer and more contemplative look at your own life. I pray and truly believe God will begin to connect the dots for you about things you may have assumed were not associated or related to each other, things that show the hand of God at work in your life. Please know this: the God and Father of our Lord Jesus whom you serve, who promised you that He would never leave you nor forsake you, has been with you through all you have encountered. May He open your eyes that you may see the hand of God in your own life.

Acknowledgments

———◆———

I'd like to thank my daughter Rachel Gaines Hockett, her husband Brian Hockett, and my two wonderful grandchildren, Olivia and Briley Hockett, who were the inspiration for this book. I also thank my sons Jason and Nathan for your love, support, and encouragement.

A special thanks to Pastors Jimmy Sargent, Dave Allman, Patrice Gordon, Merissa Davis, John Rayburn, Gerald Jordan, Chester Pipkin, Dale Evrist, Victor Torres, Rice Broocks, Steve Stells, Randy Gilbert, Rich Blue, Lawrence Lewis, James Forbes, Marty Layton, Leon Walters, Robb and Shanda Tripp, and C.S. McCall.

To those who've helped me on my journey: Ola Dandridge, Fred Hammond, Louis Upkins, David Forbes, Elizabeth Gonzales, Michael Omartian, Stormie Omartian, Da'Dra Crawford Greathouse, Kathie Lee Gifford, Christine Gardner, Greg McCollum, Chris McCollum, Angie McCollum, Marcia Lucas, Mary Sloan, Tami Jones Andrews, BJ Pons, Dawn Rix, Jackie Patillo, Sal Oliveri, Ted Theo Pearlman, Thornton Douglas Cline, Pat Holt, Irlene Mandrell, Kelly Wright, D. Scott Miller, Kathleen Hawkins, Jeff Shannon Hawkins, Lynn Bowels, Susan Hunter, Deanne DeWitt, Lorraine Morgan Scott, Cheryl Coleman Brown, Brenda Russell, Dwan K. Holmes, Nathan DiGesare, Laurie DiGesare,

Donna Summer, Bruce Sudano, Dianne Stewart, Michelle Robinson, Cheryl Puryear, Dilya Knight, Cherri Miles Patton, Lawanda Mason, Smitty David Smith, Karlton Taylor, DeMarco Johnson, Richard Felton, Derion Haynes, Greg Feste, Jed Seneca, Greg Nelson, John G. Elliott, Michael Puryear, Elwyn Raymer, Steve Lorenz, Charlie Monk, Andy Ivey, John Birdwell, Charles Dorris, Paul Smith, Joyce Hardy, Larry Sparks, Darren Tyler, Sam Chappell, Bobby Hite, Patty Leatherwood, Debbie Stevens Palmour, Nancy Harmon, Dan Cleary, Jerry Park, Mike DeMonico, Gentry McCreary, Danniebelle Hall, Charlene Johnson, Earl Fries, Mike Ballard, Kevin Diggs, Bill Smalt, Kenny Martin, Vivian Creekmoore, Rob and Maudrice Oliver, Larry Crew, Jim Michaels, Paul Rogers, Randy Bugg, Kurt Kaiser, James Bullard, Rocky, Nancy Nepola, Phil Webb, Calvin Duncan, Hardy Nickerson, Steve Parson, Horace Hockett, Bill Traylor, Jim Abernathy, Neal Joseph, Dave Jamerson, Shelly Rusk, Terri Christian, Victor Caldwell, Tess Erwin, Terry Woods, Doc Christian, Cavelle Phillips, Herb Pollard, Steve Meeks, Christy Meeks-Gaines, Terrence Allen, Barbara Eason, Yinka Danyan, Deonca Roberts, Zee Stokes, Diana Akers, Billie Ann Smith, Bram and Dianne Manusama, CeCe Winans, Olene Jordan, Lucia Sharon Hutcherson, Terry McCollam, Diana Vasquez Cox, Jordan Bobo, James Reed, Cary and Tabitha Sinnett, Larry Meeks, Rabbi Jason Sobel, Randy and Jelly Valimont, Cheryl Martin Wright, Dina Torres-Cantu de Phan, Linda Green, Marcus and Tina Wilson, Lep Andrews, John and Suzanne Spencer, Cherelle Compton, JD Compton, Reginald Washington, Greg Wilson, Chris Stafford, Rod Loy, Phil Lucas, Steve Mohn, Paula Mosher Wallace, Bruce and Yvette Vann, Mary Todd Williams, Megan Shanley, Candace Dove Benward, Senator Jack Johnson, Chris and Julie Green, Steve Houpe, Sharon Brown, Monica Winston, Charlene Tilton, and Tim Wharton.

Special thanks to Sister Ann Busby Fennel for your words of encouragement and direction.

A big thank you to Audrey Hingley for bringing my collection of memories into book form and for her husband Brian Hingley. I'd also like to thank Bayley Holt for cover and page design and my editor, Ashley Hagan, for allowing me to see just how hard an editor has to work.

Thanks to Barbara Ann Jeter and the Eternal Heiress Board (Mandy Arledge, Nise Davies, Laura Conner, Jola Moore, and Jessica Scholes) for your vision and for believing not in me necessarily, but in what our Heavenly Father had placed in me, that was purposed to be used for the furtherance of the Gospel of Jesus Christ. Also, for your substantive dedication in bringing all the elements and participants to bring this book into existence.

Thanks in memory of April Blue Taylor, whom I had so desired to see hold this book in her hands. She is now in the presence of Jesus having passed from this life on September 30, 2023. Her immeasurable contribution to the very foundation of my Christian life lives on in me.

Song References

Family History of Faith

Gaines, Sarah, "The Part that No One Sees," track 4 on *Billy & Sarah Gaines,* Benson Records, 1986, vinyl.

School Years

Sammis, John H.,"Trust and Obey,"1887.

Gaines, Billy, "Lead Me to Calvary," track 9 on *Ten Thousand Angels*, BearCub Music, 2010, compact disc.

Falling in Love

Hathaway, Donny, "For All We Know," track 6 *Roberta Flack and Donny Hathaway*, Atlantic, 1972, vinyl.

Living the Dream

Gaines, Billy, "Underlined," track 5 on Friends Indeed, Benson Records, 1990, vinyl.

Gaines, Billy and Sarah, "The One Within," track 5 on *No One Loves Me Like You*, Benson Records, 1991, vinyl.

More Open Doors

Gaines, Billy and Sarah, "The Other Side of This Trial," track 7 on *Come On Back*, BearCub Music, 1996, vinyl.

God's Goodness and Mercy

"Worship from a Wounded Heart," Copyright BearCub Music, 2019., unrecorded.

About the Author

Billy Gaines is a two-time Dove Award winner who has inspired audiences worldwide for more than four decades, spreading the gospel in song through television, radio, albums, and live performances. With the late Sarah Gaines, Billy landed a five-album deal with Benson Records in the late 80s, and rose to prominence as an R&B trailblazer, garnering six number-one singles on Contemporary Christian radio, and a number-two video on BET. Recent accomplishments are his singing/acting role in the Kathie Lee Gifford movie *The Way* as the character Moses, as well as having a number one song ("There Will Come A Day") on the 2022 European Independent Artist Airplay chart.

Scan this QR code to book Billy Gaines for singing or speaking engagements.

Eternal Heiress Publishing

Eternal Heiress Publishing is an outgrowth of Eternal Heiress Ministries, whose primary mission is to "go into all the world and preach the gospel," including into some of the darkest places. It was founded as a way to disciple, train, and mentor Christ-like character in men and women by teaching them their value and identity as Heirs of Christ. Since 2011, Eternal Heiress has ministered to the fatherless and troubled teens in detention centers in the Nashville area, where they have shared the Gospel and seen well over a thousand decisions for Christ and hundreds of baptisms. Additionally, this ministry has partnered in providing orphan care with Gospel Partners.

Eternal Heiress also has a ministry to women called Power Hour which encourages and empowers them to fulfill their unique purpose by rising up to take their royal position in God's kingdom. Like Queen Esther, they intercede and reign in life during this historic time. Power Hour also encourages women to have their own daily power hour of intercession, prayer, thanksgiving, praise, Bible study and inquiring of God. In addition, Eternal Heiress partnered to support the launch of She Leads Tennessee, which is the state chapter of She Leads America.

Eternal Heiress helped birth and is a partner ministry of King's Hill House of Prayer. Iniatiatives flowing from King's Hill House of Prayer are Pray Nashville and Pray USA:Operation Nehemiah. King's Hill Music was recently launched, and their first release, "Great, Great King," sung by Billy Gaines, recieved positive critical reviews and made it into the Top 20 World Indie & European Indie Charts.

Eternal Heiress Ministries "turns orphans into heirs." We invite you to give or get involved with this fruitful ministry. For more information, contact barbaraann@ eternalheiress.org or visit www.eternalheiress.org.